The Indomitable Spirit

PHOTOGRAPHERS AND ARTISTS
RESPOND TO THE TIME OF AIDS

The Indomitable Spirit museum tour:

February 9 - April 7, 1990
The International Center of Photography Midtown
1133 Avenue of the Americas at 43rd Street
New York, New York

May 13 - June 17, 1990
The Los Angeles Municipal Art Gallery
Barnsdall Arts Park
Los Angeles, California

Additional venues to be announced.

The works from *The Indomitable Spirit*
will be auctioned in the fall of 1990 at:

Sotheby's
1334 York Avenue
New York, New York

This catalogue has been underwritten by grants from
The Robert Mapplethorpe Foundation Inc.,
Sotheby's, and the E.T. Harimax Foundation.

PHOTOGRAPHERS + FRIENDS UNITED AGAINST AIDS

105 HUDSON STREET SUITE 208 NEW YORK CITY 10013
212 226 3430 FAX 212 219 2203

This book is published in conjunction with the exhibition
The Indomitable Spirit for the charitable and educational purposes of
Photographers + Friends United Against AIDS.
ISBN: 0-8109-2455-2

Design: Virginia Edwards
Production: Lee Goodman
Cover: John Schlesinger, Untitled, 1989 (detail, catalogue no. 26)
Frontispiece: Robert Mapplethorpe, Negro Bust, 1988 (catalogue no. 50)

The Indomitable Spirit

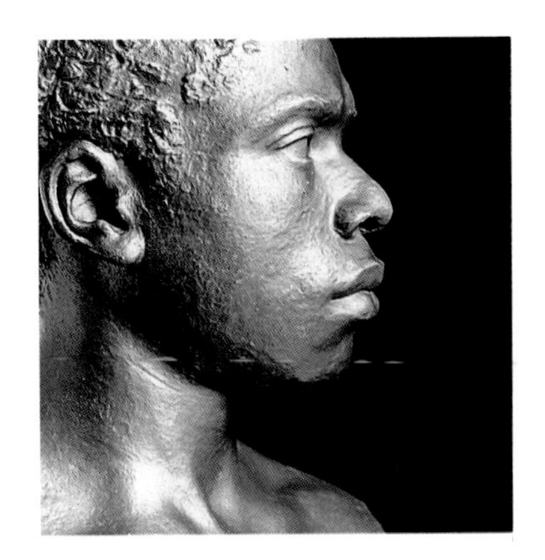

PHOTOGRAPHERS + FRIENDS UNITED AGAINST AIDS

NEW YORK 1990

DISTRIBUTED BY HARRY N. ABRAMS, INC., NEW YORK

PHOTOGRAPHERS + FRIENDS UNITED AGAINST AIDS

Photographers + Friends United Against AIDS is a not-for-profit corporation committed to fighting a deadly epidemic that has, directly or indirectly, affected us all. The goal of the organization is to stimulate awareness and action through photographic imagery and to raise significant new funds from the art and photographic community to benefit AIDS care, research, and education.

Photographers + Friends' program, to our knowledge, is the first effort to unite the diverse elements of the photography community – commercial photographers, art photographers, fashion photographers, sports photographers, photojournalists, artists, and scientists who use photography – to come together in common cause. *The Indomitable Spirit* exhibition represents their positive contribution to this overwhelming crisis.

Each program of Photographers + Friends has been designed to raise awareness among a broad audience as well as to raise funds. Photographers + Friends' programs include *The Indomitable Spirit* museum exhibition, the production and sale of a limited edition portfolio, and this catalogue, as well as a series of postcards and posters. The works from the exhibition will be auctioned at Sotheby's New York in the fall of 1990. Funds raised from these programs will be distributed to two national AIDS organizations – the National Community AIDS Partnership (NCAP) and the American Foundation for AIDS Research (AmFAR). Additionally, *The Indomitable Spirit* museum exhibition will serve as a centerpiece for fund-raising events to benefit regional AIDS organizations in the cities where it is shown.

Lisa Cremin
Executive Director

The pictures you are about to see represent an attempt to harness the power of photography to inspire each of us to act with optimism and compassion and energy to meet the many challenges presented by the AIDS epidemic.

The Indomitable Spirit was born out of sadness, loss, and the frustration that accompanies inaction. After losing over two dozen friends and acquaintances to this disease, I felt it was time to enlist the talent and energy of friends in photography to inspire action and raise funds to support the varied efforts to combat AIDS.

Each of us will react to these images personally and uniquely. I hope that at least one of them will speak to you directly or metaphorically. We hope you will leave this exhibition wanting to become involved in the efforts to lessen the devastating impact of this disease. An index in this catalogue lists some of the organizations, national and local, that can provide AIDS information. If you have not already been touched by AIDS the chances are that as time passes, you will be. Either directly, through the illness and death of friends or loved ones, or indirectly, through the impact AIDS is having on our national health care programs and facilities, the epidemic affects us all.

This project could not have been completed without the generosity and support of the exhibition participants; the institutions where *The Indomitable Spirit* will be presented; and the private, foundation, and corporate sponsorships we have received. Photographers + Friends United Against AIDS thanks all those who have helped us toward achieving our goal.

To care is to become involved.

Joseph Hartney
Founder, President of the Board of Directors

PREFACE

The notion of assembling a collection of photographs that "celebrate human strength, compassion, and endurance in the face of challenge and adversity"– the words curator Marvin Heiferman used in his prospectus to the artists participating in this project – is ambitious and, in a sense, presumptuous. It presumes that photographs have the power to move us, to stir our emotions, and to give us solace at a time when solace is in remarkably short supply.

For more than 100 years, photographers have aspired to move us with their pictures. In the nineteenth century, Thomas Annan in Britain and Jacob Riis in the United States sought to create a public awareness of urban ills. In our century, Lewis Hine is perhaps the best known example of a photographer who consciously and conscientiously attempted to change the social order through photographs. In part, he succeeded; his pictures of children working in coal mines and textile mills helped move Congress to pass the first child labor law.

Often photographs work in mysterious ways. Carleton Watkins's pictures of Yosemite Valley, for example, helped convince Congress in 1864 to make the area a national park; Watkins's intention, however, was merely to record its beauty. More recently, photographs by Andres Serrano and Robert Mapplethorpe have spurred Congress to place restrictions on the National Endowment for the Arts. It seems obvious that photographs can be important tools in shaping political opinion, sometimes in spite of themselves.

How camera images affect us is a complex, never ending issue. The French critic Roland Barthes, in his book *Camera Lucida,* noted that the emotional impact of photographs often is incidental to their main subjects. Another way to describe this phenomenon is to say that the pleasures or pains we derive from looking at photographs rarely coincide with the intentions of their makers. As signs, photographs are unruly; they seem to want to escape the bounds of conventional meaning, to leave reality behind in favor of metaphor.

Today, when the conventions of well intended documentary photography seem exhausted, metaphor serves an important purpose. It enables photographers and artists who make use of photographs to exceed the boundaries of camera description, to create images that are less illustrative than suggestive. This may explain why many of the images here, dedicated to "the indomitable spirit," appear to be focused on more prosaic matters. Like the idea of spirit itself, their subject can only be described metaphorically.

It may at first appear preposterous, in the age of AIDS, to focus on that part of the human spirit that perseveres. To some, the idea may smack of *The Family of Man,* an exhibition that erased social and cultural realities in its resolution to remain upbeat. To others, it may seem naive, given the ongoing critique of how AIDS has been represented (or, more accurately, misrepresented) within American society. But we may already have seen too many photographs of the havoc of the disease, too many depressing visions of its ravages. To many of us in the art world, no photographic images of AIDS itself are really necessary: we see the toll of AIDS in its human form, among our friends and families.

In *Camera Lucida,* Barthes concludes that ultimately photographs are signs of what once was, that they always intimate our own death. It is ironic, then, that here photography is enlisted against death, as a tonic for the spiritual miasma that hangs over all of us who live in the age of AIDS. But the pictures of *The Indomitable Spirit* are also testimony to the complex and sometimes confounding possibilities of photographic meaning, and to the ingenuity and courage of their makers. By their mere existence, these photographs are incontrovertible evidence of the spirit they attempt to make visible.

Andy Grundberg

INTRODUCTION

MARVIN HEIFERMAN

The AIDS virus is coursing through the bloodstream of our lives. People with AIDS and the HIV virus live in a precariously tenuous state: hope is balanced against fear, energy against exhaustion, resolve against despair. Those who are not ill, and those who are not ill yet, worry. If a cold lingers too long, we are certain that we're dying. When a skin rash appears, it's *Kaposi's sarcoma.* We flip through newspapers and scan the obituary columns to see who has died too young or without mention of the cause of death. There are even times when we fear that the blinking light on the answering machine is counting out another loss.

By 1991, AIDS is predicted to be the leading cause of death among Americans aged 25 to 44. And, as the death count climbs, our fear turns to anger. An intense anger against a government that spends too little money, too slowly. An intense anger at the drug companies that overcharge for the few medications available. An intense anger at those individuals who, in the name of religion or politics, obstruct education and prevention programs to help stop the spread of the disease. We are furious with people who believe that AIDS is a punishment; these people are wrong. Not a single infant, child, woman or man, heterosexual or homosexual, movie star, politician, American or African or European or Asian, not a single drug user, teacher, priest, policeman, neighbor, or stranger who is ill with AIDS deserves to die.

AIDS is devastating our communities, our workplaces, our health care systems, our economies, our cultures, our world, and our future. In its face, we must take action; we must scream and fight. We must donate money, and we must volunteer our services.

And, unfortunately, we must endure. The battle against AIDS will be a protracted struggle.

We have already experienced signs of optimism. The first drug therapies have been discovered, and new medications are being tested. Better care facilities are being built. Millions of dollars are being spent. But this is not enough. Each new round of alarming statistics underscores the fact that the victory against AIDS has yet to come. No matter how hard some of us are trying, more of us must work even harder. Courage, strength, and compassion continue to be tested. In that process, we must also maintain hope.

Hope is at the heart of *The Indomitable Spirit.* For this exhibition, leading members of the photography and art communities were asked to contribute an image that affirmed the human will to live, one that celebrated human endurance and resiliency in the face of overwhelming obstacles. Bound together by the powerful language of photography, the participants in the project include commercial photographers, art photographers, fashion photographers, sports photographers, and photojournalists, as well as artists who use photography and scientists who depend on it for research. Each has donated a work that reveals his or her thoughts, methods of working, and most importantly, feelings. Their choices are unusual, moving, beautiful, intelligent, and provocative.

Consciously, *The Indomitable Spirit* is not an exhibition of photographs of people with AIDS. In recent years, such photographic exhibitions have been mounted in galleries, museums, and community spaces. Some have been controversial. Shocking, confrontational portraits did make AIDS graphic and telegraphed the terrifying reality of the disease to a public that previously was indifferent. But loud concern was voiced that these pictures of people with AIDS were voyeuristic, exploitative, and morally wrong. In response, more exhibitions were mounted, urging viewers to understand the precise ethical, social, medical, and political issues that underlie the complicated AIDS crisis.

It is the goal of Photographers + Friends United Against AIDS that *The Indomitable Spirit* address a different aspect of the impact of AIDS on our lives. The project is designed to harness the rich, communicative power of photography to honor the determination and perseverance of those who are ill and to help raise substantial funds for AIDS research, patient care, and education. The underlying concept uses photography to unite people emotionally and not to separate illness from health, or draw distinctions between "us" and "them."

When we asked each participant to create a new work or to select an image to commemorate human resourcefulness, we knew it would not be a simple task. Many of the photographers and artists whose lives have been directly affected by the AIDS crisis found it impossible to produce unqualified, positive visual statements. Most had gone through the experience of having someone close to them die. Some feared becoming ill; some already were. To the photographers and artists whose lives are, as yet, safe from AIDS, the project created a different challenge: to make a visual statement that expresses concern and support that is authentic. Intense self-questioning and tests of empathy were required.

The works these men and women provided are as surprising as the range of artistic solutions is wide. In this sense, *The Indomitable Spirit* is a celebration of photographic invention and an expression of the photography community's deepest desire that the medium be used to affect change. There is much to be learned from these pictures – about photography and about caring. It is our hope that these images will work to make each of us reflect upon the dignity of human life and then to act. Passivity, the feeling of being victimized or overwhelmed, will not end the AIDS crisis. It will take the exertion of our own authority, the insistence that we each have the imagination and the power to save lives, to find the cure for AIDS, to give those in need the best care humanly possible, and to change the course of history.

PHOTOGRAPHS IN THE EXHIBITION

Captions: Marvin Heiferman

1.

1.
GENERAL IDEA

IMAGE VIRUS

Chromogenic development print (Ektacolor). 1989. Signed, dated, and numbered 1/6 on the verso. 30 x 20 in. Donated by the artists, courtesy Koury Wingate Gallery.

General Idea, a collaborative group, creates posters, stickers, and mass transit placards that take Robert Indiana's familiar "LOVE" painting and substitute the word "AIDS" for "LOVE." By placing this seemingly cheerful image in public passageways, it hopes to jolt viewers into recognizing the widespread problems AIDS raises for each of us. And how, like love, AIDS will not disappear.

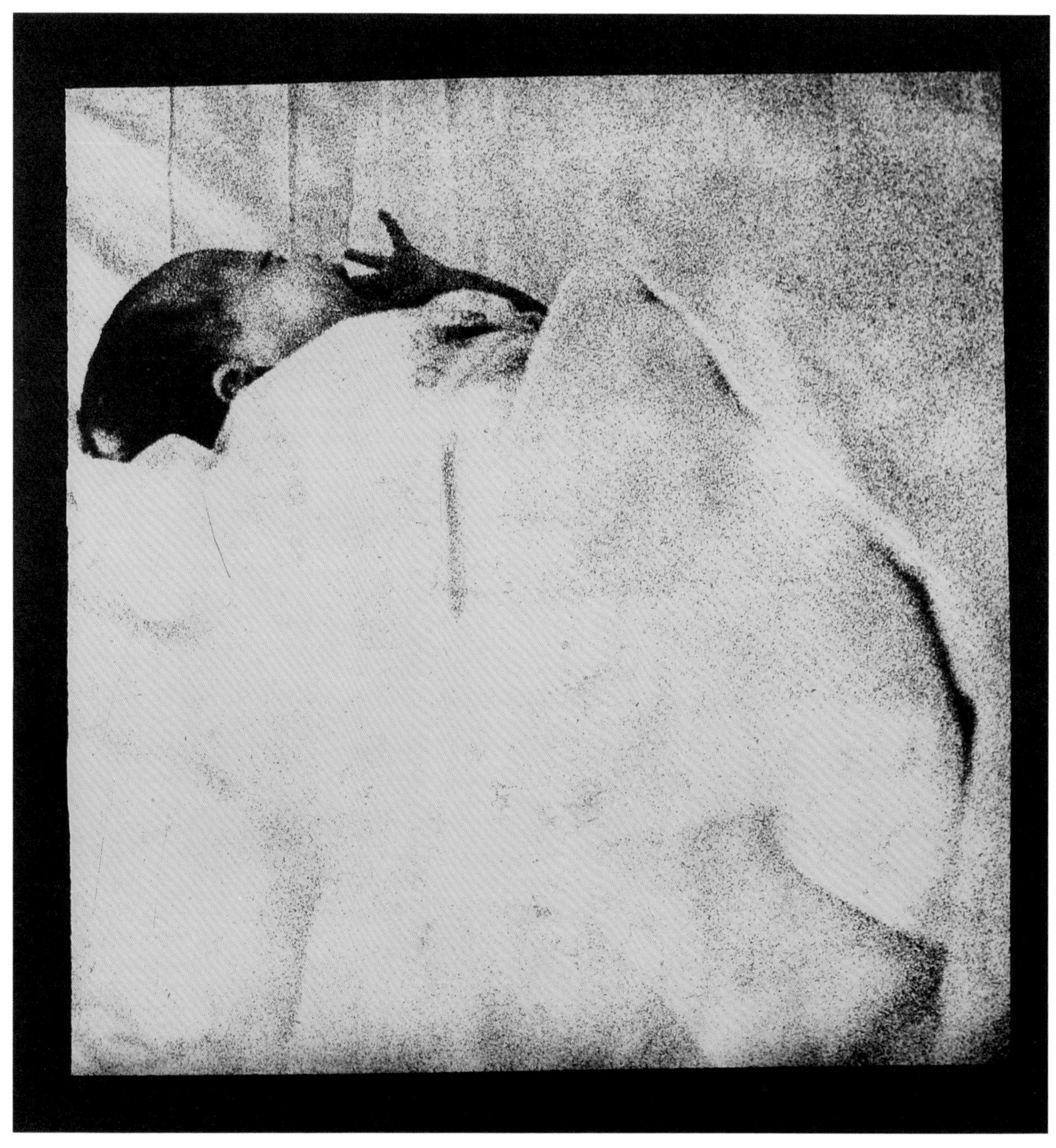

2.

2.
BRIAN WEIL

7 DAY OLD CHILD WITH AIDS

Gelatin silver print. 1989. Signed, titled, and numbered 3/3 in pencil in the margin. 42 x 42 in.
Donated by the artist.

A few years ago, Weil began work as a volunteer in an AIDS program. His interests and his work shifted radically, from documenting sex acts and murders to recording the lives of people with AIDS. He was instrumental in establishing the first infants' AIDS program in New York City and is compiling a series of portraits of children, families, and adults whose lives have been affected by AIDS. His photographs stress the spirituality of their subjects rather than dwelling on the physical manifestations of the disease. This is a photograph of an HIV-positive infant.

3.

3.
ANN MEREDITH

MEREDITH WITH HER MOTHER LILLIAN

Gelatin silver print. 1988. From the series *Until That Last Breath, Women with AIDS.* Signed in ink on the recto. 31 1/2 x 44 1/2 in. Donated by the artist.

As part of her documentation of women with AIDS, Ann Meredith has made tape recordings of her subjects:
Meredith: If I tell you that I was diagnosed with a terminal illness, the normal reaction is: "How are you feeling?" If I say I have AIDS, the first question I get is "How'd you get it?" You hear AIDS and have a pre-conceived idea of lifestyle and morality. What is my crime? That I loved somebody too much? A little too ignorantly?
Lillian: How do I feel about Merry being sick? I feel it's just dreadful. Something must be done, there must be a cure. I think the important thing is to let them (people with AIDS) know you love them, verbally and physically. The love continues, it doesn't stop.

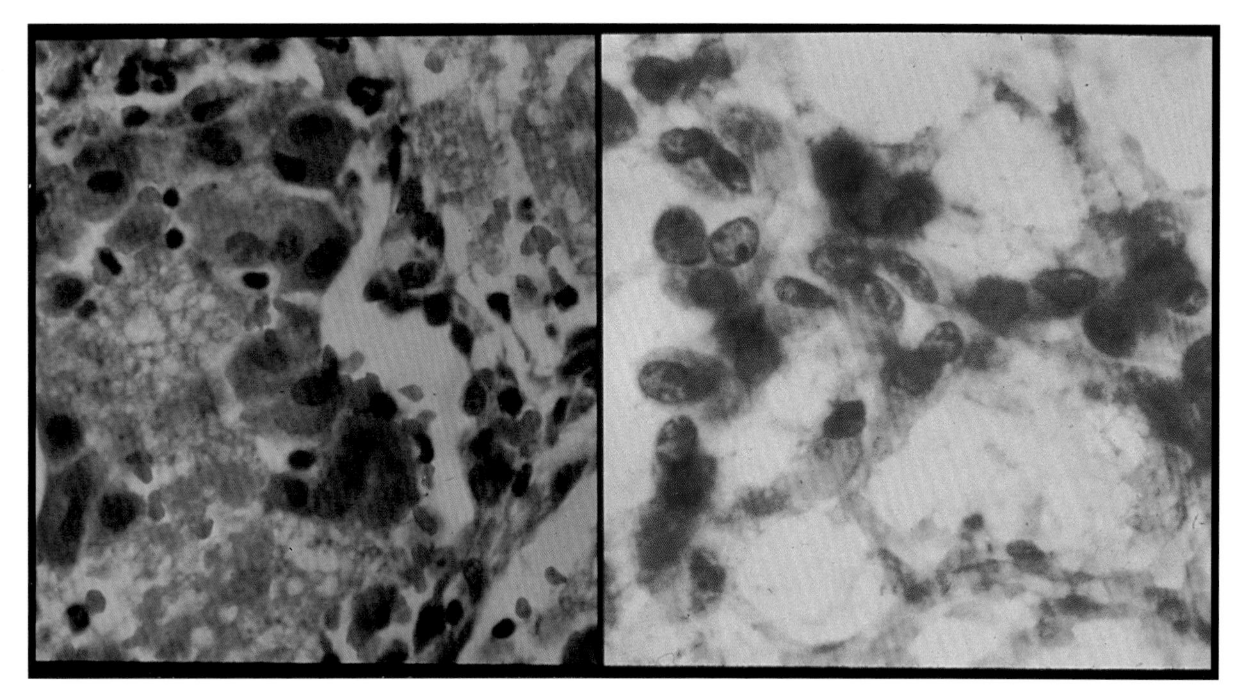

4 . (detail)

4 .
NANCY BURSON

VISUALIZATION IMAGES FOR AIDS-RELATED PNEUMONIA

Chromogenic development print (Ektacolor).
1988. Signed and dated in ink, with copyright stamp on the verso. 16 x 20 in. Donated by the artist, courtesy Jayne Baum Gallery.

After the deaths of both her mother and a close friend, Burson (known for her computer-altered portraits) began to make photographic images that could be employed in visualization healing techniques. Persons who are ill are encouraged to study photographs carefully, to concentrate, and to reflect on the visual differences between healthy (left) and diseased (right) tissues as a means of psychologically and physically empowering themselves toward recovery.

5.

5.
LYNN DAVIS

ICEBURG, DISKO BAY

Silver dye bleach print (Cibachrome). 1986. 40 x 30 in.
Signed on the verso. Donated by the artist.

Beauty and danger tend to co-exist in pictures a bit more comfortably than they do in life. It's the case in this photograph, made by Davis off the Greenland coast. It is a clear, cool, beautiful image, and it might be read as a metaphor for AIDS. The huge, destructive power of an iceberg lies under the water's surface, just as the true dimensions of the AIDS crisis still remain hidden, below the fragile fabric of society.

7.

6.

6.
MITCH EPSTEIN

CRICKET MATCH

Chromogenic development print (Ektacolor). 1987.
Signed, titled, and dated in ink on the verso.
14 3/4 x 21 7/8 in. Donated by the artist.

In this photograph, taken in Grenada, lightness balances with darkness and life is, quite literally, played out in the face of death. A group of men are taking a break in a graveyard, and the tombstones marking individual graves become a grandstand. From their new vantage points, the game of life can be seen and, perhaps, better understood.

8.

7.
LEE FRIEDLANDER

SONORAN DESERT

Gelatin silver print. 1988. Signed, titled, and dated in pencil, with photographer's copyright stamp on the verso. 10 3/8 x 15 5/8 in. Donated by the artist.

That certain plants, animals, and organisms survive in inhospitable environments is a testimony to biological adjustment. In his celebrated street pictures, Friedlander shows us how to navigate a path through a tangle of urban visual information. In this image, he celebrates the adaptive powers we draw on every day.

8.
DUANE MICHALS

THE MOMENT OF TRUTH

Gelatin silver print. 1989. Signed and numbered 1/25 in ink on the recto. 6 3/4 x 10 in. Donated by the artist.

In Dante's *Inferno,* a complex system of eternal punishments was meted out to those who had broken society's codes. In Michals's photograph, the moral structures of fiction are separated from the pressing reality of AIDS. AIDS is not a punishment. It is a virus that operates without conscience. Unlike Dante and Virgil, who appear in the background as silent observers, it is our responsibility to take action, to fight for change.

10.

9.

9.

LINDA CONNOR

DOTS AND HANDS, FOURTEEN WINDOW RUIN, UTAH

Toned gelatin silver print. 1987. Signed, titled, and dated in pencil on the verso. 7 1/2 x 9 7/8 in.
Donated by the artist.

A survey of mark-making, one that began with the Lascaux cave drawings and extends to today's spray-painted graffiti, would reveal that at every level of civilization people feel a need to leave behind a permanent and public record of their existence. Connor, who has photographed rock art sites for years, made this image at an eleventh century Pueblo dwelling site, near the San Juan River.

11.

10.
JOHN GUTMANN

SIGNALS: "SELF"

Gelatin silver print. 1987. Signed, titled and dated in pencil on the verso. 10 3/16 x 13 1/8 in. Donated by the artist.

This image is both a document of the street and a proud proclamation. Gutmann, who fled to the United States from Germany in 1933, continues to be interested in the outspokenness of Americans. He lives in San Francisco, a city particularly hard struck by AIDS, where this image could read as a sign of respect for the community's tenacity and caring.

11.
CINDY SHERMAN

UNTITLED

Chromogenic development print (Ektacolor). 1979. Printed later. Signed in ink on the verso. 21 3/16 x 29 1/16 in. Donated by the artist, courtesy Metro Pictures.

Sherman's first self-portraits were made more than a decade ago, as a response to the stereotyped portrayals of women in the media. In this photograph – the only color image from that body of work – she appears as a very modern indomitable spirit, the slightly startled suburban woman who will not, in all probability, be stopped from doing her nails.

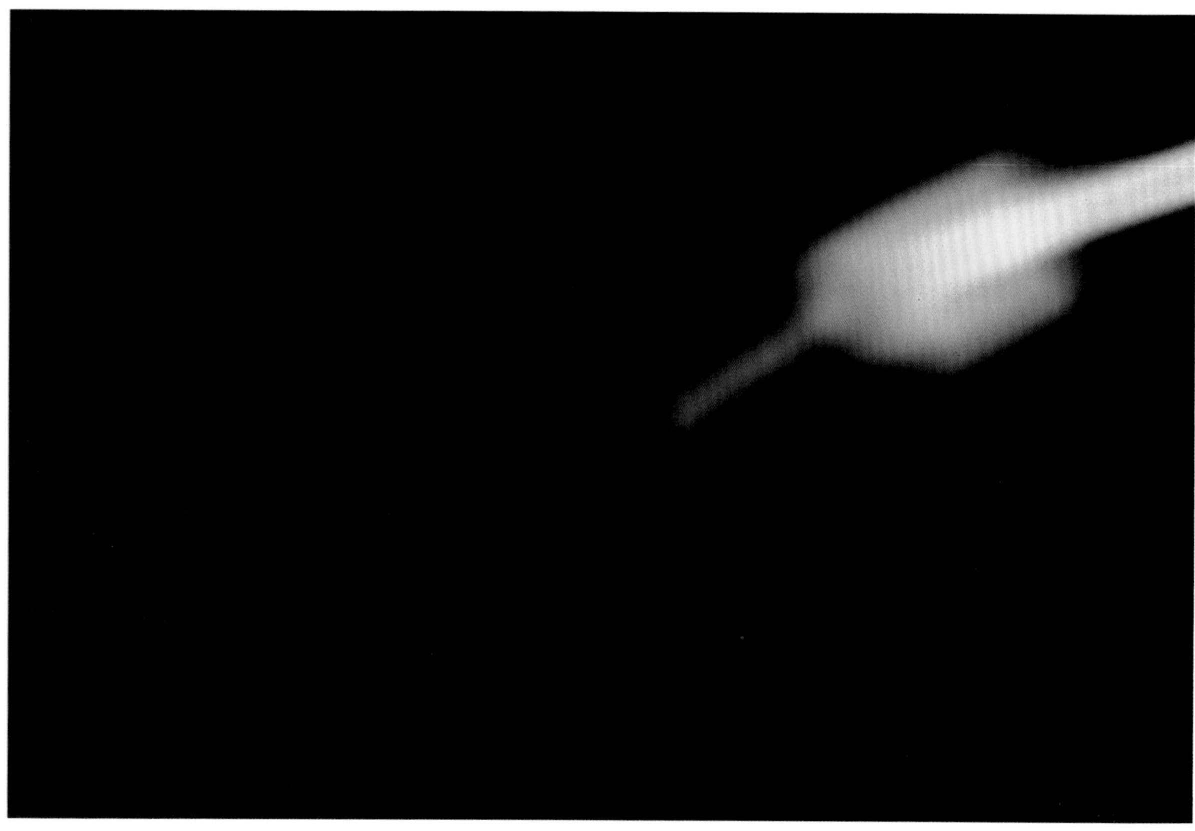

12.

12.
ANDRES SERRANO

UNTITLED III

Silver dye bleach print (Cibachrome). 1989. Signed on the verso. 40 x 60 in. Donated by the artist, courtesy Stux Gallery.

Serrano's earliest photographic works, theatrically staged religious tableaux, were the first step in an ongoing exploration of ritual and faith. Recently, he has made graphic images in which bodily fluids, such as blood, milk, and urine, are presented as the corporeal manifestations of spirit. In this photograph of semen, two simultaneous facts heighten the tension raised by the subject matter; the bodily fluid that contributes to life can, as one carrier of the AIDS virus, also contribute to death.

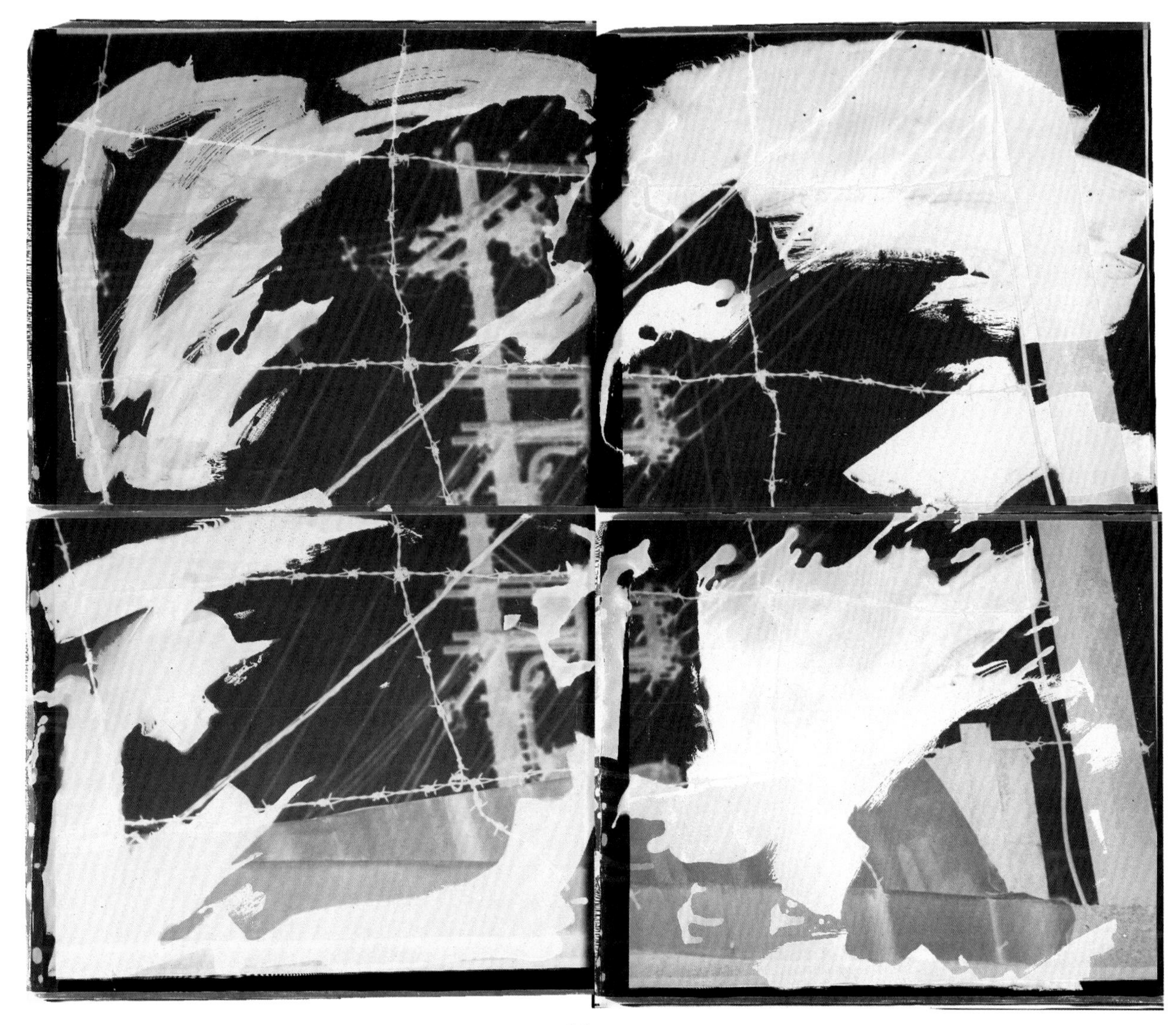

13.

13.
ROBERT RAUSCHENBERG

UNTITLED (FROM THE BLEACHERS SERIES)

Four bleached silver gelatin transfer prints. Mounted on aluminum. 1989. 45 1/2 x 55 in. Signed in ink on the recto. Donated by the artist, courtesy Pace/MacGill.

In classical mythology, Sisyphus was condemned to perpetually roll a stone up a hill. The repetitious quality of our everyday lives often makes us feel equally burdened. Rauschenberg, in this multiple image work, seems to offer a suggestion. Using bleach, he has reworked each of the identical photographs, proposing that through enthusiasm, creativity, and persistence, the mundane can be made unique and fresh.

14.

14.
TINA BARNEY

THE WATCH

Chromogenic development print (Ektacolor). 1985.
Signed in ink on the recto. 46 x 57 in.
Donated by the artist, courtesy Janet Borden, Inc.

The art on the wall (an early Picasso painting) is supposed to last forever. The flower arrangement placed before it will probably die within the week. Shortly before her marriage, a woman and her brother are momentarily absorbed in private thoughts that echo the symbolism of their surroundings. The bride stares at a ring that stands for a union meant to last forever. The brother looks at the watch that isolates the present from the past and always promises a future.

15.

15.
JUDITH ROSS

LITTLE BOY WITH HIS BIKE

Toned gelatin silver print. 1988. Signed, titled, and dated in pencil on the verso. 9 5/8 x 7 5/8 in.
Donated by the artist.

A boy tests his bravery and sense of balance against the force of gravity. Although the kickstand is down, the bike leans precariously. The odds are even that the kid will stand up or fall down. In either case, he will probably try his balancing act again, because when children experiment and play, the element of risk is often the best part of the game.

16.

17.

16.
DORIT CYPIS

RECOVERY

Two silver dye bleach prints (Cibachrome), wood, and brass easel. 1989. Signed on reverse of the frame. 20 x 60 in. and 4 x 6 in. Donated by the artist.

The frame is a proscenium. The light in the large photograph is a deep, cinematic blue. The setting is pure theater in which an anonymous, female nude in silhouette reclines. This large picture is the story. On a small easel, in front of this backdrop, a second photograph shows a nude woman, sitting up. She can be seen in the light. She has a face, a body, and she touches herself. This picture is the fact. Each is a part of Cypis's self-portrait, which acknowledges the difficulty of identifying the sense of one's body in the age of AIDS.

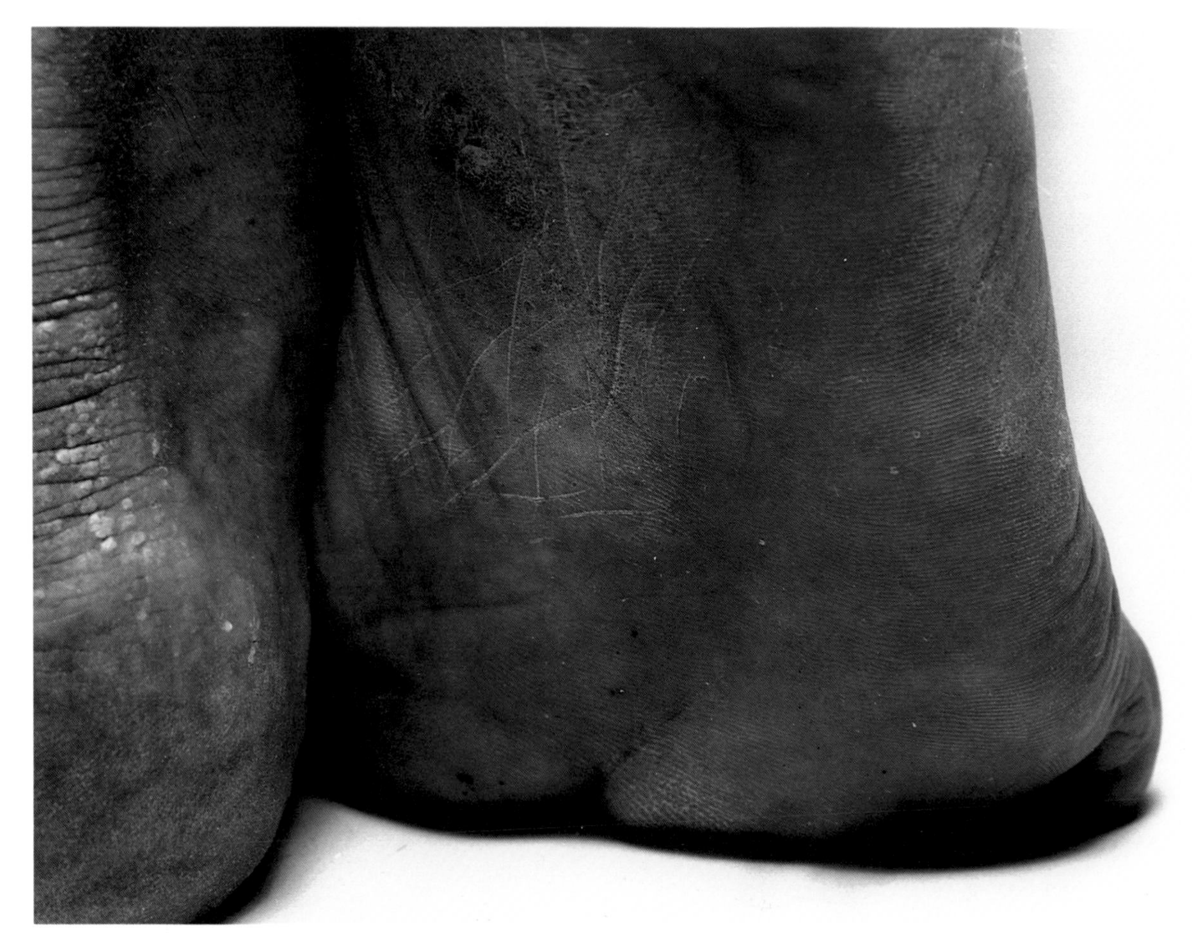

18.

17.
CARL FISCHER

UNTITLED

Collage of chromogenic development prints (Ektacolor). 1989. Signed in pencil on the recto, with the artist's copyright stamp on the verso. 20 3/4 x 16 3/4 in. Donated by the artist.

In this collage, Fischer presents an illustration of a fairy tale gone wrong. The handsome young man gazing in the mirror cannot see his smooth reflection. He sees a skull. In the time of AIDS, his story can have only two happy endings. In the first, he finds the resources and strength to live in the face of death. In the second, a cure for AIDS is discovered.

18.
JOHN COPLANS

SELF PORTRAIT (FOOT)

Gelatin silver print. 1989. Signed in pencil on the verso. 29 3/4 x 39 3/4 in. Donated by the artist.

A number of years ago, Coplans, who had already been a museum director, an editor of *Artforum,* and a critic of contemporary painting and sculpture, chose to become a photographer. His most recent photographs are a series of self-portraits. They are neither glamorous nor overwrought; they are often confrontational, forcing viewers to acknowledge and accept the body's physical changes that come with age.

19.

19.
FRANK MAJORE

POPPIES

Silver dye bleach print (Cibachrome). 1989.
Signed, dated, and numbered 2/5 on the verso. 23 x 19 in.
Donated by the artist, courtesy Holly Solomon Gallery.

Three poppies, supported by strong and prominent stamens, are seen in contrast with a lurid, threatening sky. Majore's flowers suggest the cycle of life, in which one generation seeds the next. The whiteness of the flowers symbolizes innocence and purity, the green stems growth and vitality, the purple and pink of the sky a danger that will pass.

20.

20.
JEFF KOONS

MYCHAL

Photolithographic poster. 1985. 36 x 21 3/4 in.
Donated by the artist, courtesy Sonnabend Gallery.

Innocent play was transformed into professional sport centuries ago. In Hellenic and early Central American cultures, the great athletes were heroes. Today, they have become businessmen. Koons reminds us that while atheletic skill is still tied to heroism and mythology, our culture boosts indomitable spirits of sports into the realms of celebrity and finance as well.

21.

21.
PETE TURNER

STONEHENGE

Dye imbibition print (Dye transfer). 1979. Signed in pencil with the artist's blind stamp in the margin. 6 x 9 in. Donated by the artist, courtesy The Image Bank, New York.

Archaeologists have devoted lifetimes to cracking the riddle of Stonehenge. The circular arrangement of megalithic stones, built and rebuilt over a thousand-year period, has been thought to have been a burial ground, a cremation site, and a location for celebrations of heavenly sightings. Turner, whose color work has profoundly influenced commercial and industrial photography, captures the symbolic mystery of the site seen at sunset and under a full moon.

22.

22.
RALPH GIBSON

UNTITLED (FROM THE SERIES ARTIFACTS)

Silver gelatin print. 1981. Signed, dated, and numbered 3/25 in ink on the recto. 17 1/2 x 11 3/4 in. Donated by the artist.

A portrait is being drawn by a street artist and, as in many of Gibson's works, it is photographed with an elegance touched with surrealism. Without a view of the subject, it is impossible to tell if the likeness is a good one. But the alert eyes of the image suggest the curiosity of someone who sits down briefly to see how his portrait turns out, before he moves on to other things.

23.

23.
IRVING PENN

OLD MAN, DAHOMEY

Platinum-palladium print. 1967. Printed later. Signed, titled, dated, and numbered 11/16 in pencil, the photographer's Condé Nast copyright and edition stamps on verso. 15 3/8 x 15 in. Donated by the artist, courtesy Pace/MacGill Gallery.

Presented with the succinct beauty that characterizes Penn's work, this *Old Man* looks far beyond the border of the image. His gaze is intense. It is as if, from the privilege of advanced age, his experience and vision can accept and accommodate an understanding of the past, the present, and the future. His exotic "otherness" suggests something else; customs and beliefs bind generations together to insure the continuity of life.

24.

24.

JOHN BALDESSARI

TWO WINDOWS

Gelatin silver print, color photograph, vinyl paint. 1988.
32 x 18 in. Donated by the artist,
courtesy Sonnabend Gallery.

Through a juxtaposition of photographic images, Baldessari conceptually unites two disparate ideas about our search for knowledge and meaning. Scientific inquiry opens one window to discovery; a single new fact can literally illuminate a field of darkness. A sharing of feelings provides a second window of hope. By strengthening communal bonds, a structure for belief and a mechanism for change can be maintained.

25.

26.

25.
BARBARA ESS

UNTITLED

Monochrome chromogenic development print (Ektacolor). 1989. Certificate of authenticity. 18 3/4 x 43 1/4 in. Donated by the artist, courtesy Curt Marcus Gallery.

In this diptych, the wild force of nature is contrasted with the equally wild spirit of an animal trying to free itself from posts and wires. Taken together, the two images, blurry and heavy with their tinted atmosphere, suggest a primeval struggle of will pushing against restraint. Although it is impossible to know what might have happened in the next instant, we could choose to believe that the horse jumped the fence.

26.
JOHN SCHLESINGER

UNTITLED

Toned gelatin silver print. 1989. Signed, dated, and numbered 2/3 in pencil in the margin and signed again on the verso. 19 3/4 x 66 in. Donated by the artist.

Many of the images of danger, bravery, and strength that we carry in our minds first entered our consciousness as we sat in the dark, watching movies. Very often, it is in movie theaters that Schlesinger creates his work. He photographs pictures from the screen and then, without advancing the film fully, shoots again, to make a multiple exposure. His final prints often look like fragments from detective films. In this photograph, the beaker and searchlight suggest the suspense we experience as the search for an AIDS cure continues.

28.

27.

27.
BERT STERN

ELIZABETH TAYLOR, ROME, 1962

Gelatin silver print. 1988. Signed and dated with the photographer's copyright stamp in ink on the verso. 12 x 10 in. Donated by the artist.

There are a few public figures who not only capture our attention but truly seem to live in it. This group includes politicians, criminals, and in the past decade business-men. But actors and actresses fascinate us the most. They act out the lives of others for a fee, then live out their own lives, at a personal cost, in the glare of the media. Stern's portrait of Taylor evokes her triumphs, troubles, and stamina. We are also reminded that she continues to use her visibility to help others with her support in the fight against AIDS.

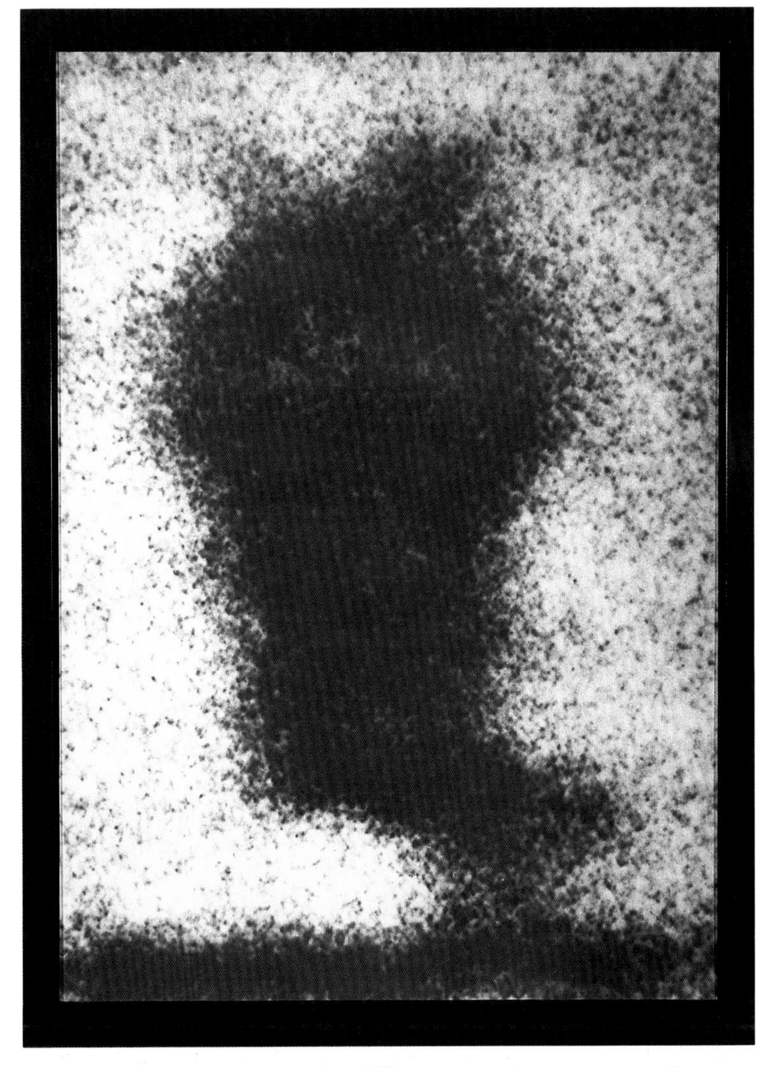

29.

29. (source photo)

28.
ROBERT HEINECKEN

UNTITLED NEWSWOMEN: CONNIE CHUNG

Jetgraph print. 1985. Signed, titled, and dated in pencil on the recto. 20 x 24 in. Donated by the artist, courtesy Pace/MacGill Gallery.

Surveys reveal that television is the major source of information and news for most Americans. The medium's bias toward entertainment – the "soft" reporting on issues such as AIDS or the well-meaning but misfocused "docu-dramas" on the disease, for example – is a hidden subject of Heinecken's photograph.

29.
ALLAN MC COLLUM

PERPETUAL PHOTO #182

Toned gelatin silver print. 1982-89. Signed in ink with the source photo affixed to the verso. 56 x 42 in.
Donated by the artist, courtesy John Weber Gallery.

There are certain people who search for art everywhere. To make his "Perpetual Photos," McCollum photographs his television screen when framed works of art appear on walls, as part of the scenery. The image of that art, cropped out of the photograph, is then radically enlarged and becomes a new and abstract work of art. Then we, as observers, scrutinize the final picture, searching for the meaning in art as intently as we search for meaning in life.

30.

30.
SANDY SKOGLUND

GERMS ARE EVERYWHERE

Silver dye bleach print (Cibachrome). 1984. Signed, dated, and numbered HC 2/5 in ink in the margin. 30 x 40 in. Donated by the artist, courtesy Lorence Monk Gallery.

It is interesting to consider that we feel most able to confront our worst fears when they are played out as entertainment. As children, we loved the irrational violence in cartoons. As teenagers, we screamed and then laughed at horror movies. As adults, we embrace the surrealism of science fiction. It is from this symbolic universe that Skoglund's work draws its vocabulary and its humor. In this exaggerated tableau, we are secretly thrilled by the fat woman's nonchalance, wishing that we could be as cool in our world, which also seems to have run amok.

31.

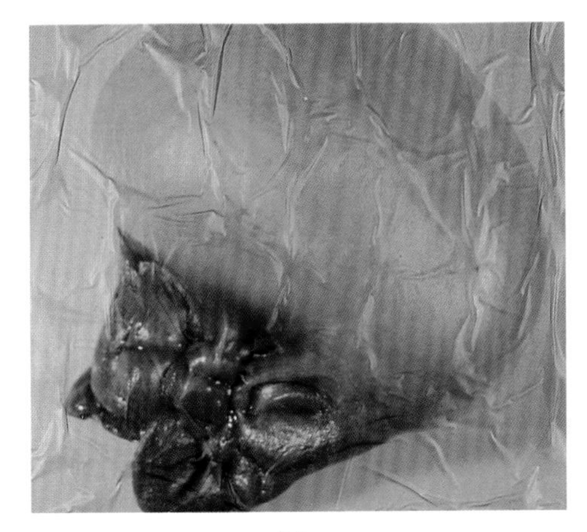

32.

31.
LARRY CLARK

UNTITLED

Three gelatin silver prints. 1989. Each signed in pencil on the verso. 12 1/4 x 8 1/8 in. each. Donated by the artist.

Teenagers investigate their interests, explore new feelings, and test social and sexual behaviors within the closed circle of their peers. Clark's triptych raises an issue of pressing importance: the need to devise and support responsible AIDS education programs that are specifically tailored for an adolescent audience.

32
ALAN BELCHER

CAVITY

Laminated silver dye bleach print (Cibachrome). 1989. Mounted on plywood with chewing gum. Signed, titled, and dated in ink on the verso. 24 x 24 in. Donated by the artist, courtesy Josh Baer Gallery.

In 1979, Mrs. Susan Montgomery Williams of California blew the largest bubble ever measured, 19 1/4 inches in diameter. None of us have matched her achievement, but we recognize the motivation, the challenge to push something as far as it will go. In this piece, Alan Belcher pushes photography, and a metaphor, into the realm of sculpture.

33.

33.
ROSALIND SOLOMON

BARBARA BRUCE, MEDICAL DOCTOR, (ATTACKED BY A SHARK IN 1963), SOUTH AFRICA, 1988

Gelatin silver print. 1988. Signed on the verso.
36 x 36 in. Donated by the artist, courtesy Robert Burge 20th Century Photographs, Ltd.

After completing a series of controversial portraits of people with AIDS, Solomon made a number of visits to South Africa, where she took photographs of the people she met. At first glance, this image of a woman on a sandy beach seems pleasant enough. But upon a second look, it becomes clear that this smiling woman has no right hand or foot. And recognizing that startling fact, we pay much closer attention to the picture, to its subject, and to its title, sensing that we are looking at a woman who embodies resiliency and fierce dedication.

34.

34.
JAN GROOVER

UNTITLED

Chromogenic development print (Ektacolor). 1989. Mounted on aluminum. Signed and dated in ink on the recto. 28 1/4 x 36 1/2 in. Donated by the artist, courtesy Robert Miller Gallery.

This beautiful, dense still life can be read on many levels. Two arms reach upwards; a gun, various bottles, a glass, and two arrangements of fruit rest on table tops supported by columns. There are signs of life, intimations of mortality, and disembodied gestures of yearning and need. Still, as loaded as these clues are, the picture remains an exquisite mystery.

35.

35.
SUSAN RANKAITIS

SCRAPING SURFACE

Combined medium on photographic paper. 1987. Signed in pencil on the verso. 80 1/2 x 49 7/8 in.
Donated by the artist, courtesy Meyers/Bloom Gallery.

This piece is the final work from a series in which Rankaitis has metaphorically honored the courage, struggle, intellectual life, and eventual death of her close friend, Roger Horwitz. He and his lover, Paul Monette, worked with Rainkaitis to create the abstract images that would eventually be incorporated in the series. This work was begun on the first anniversary of Horwitz's death from AIDS. At that time, Rankaitis inserted a profile of Monette into the piece. The work's only figurative element, it commemorates the friendship they all shared, a relationship that continues to influence her work.

36.

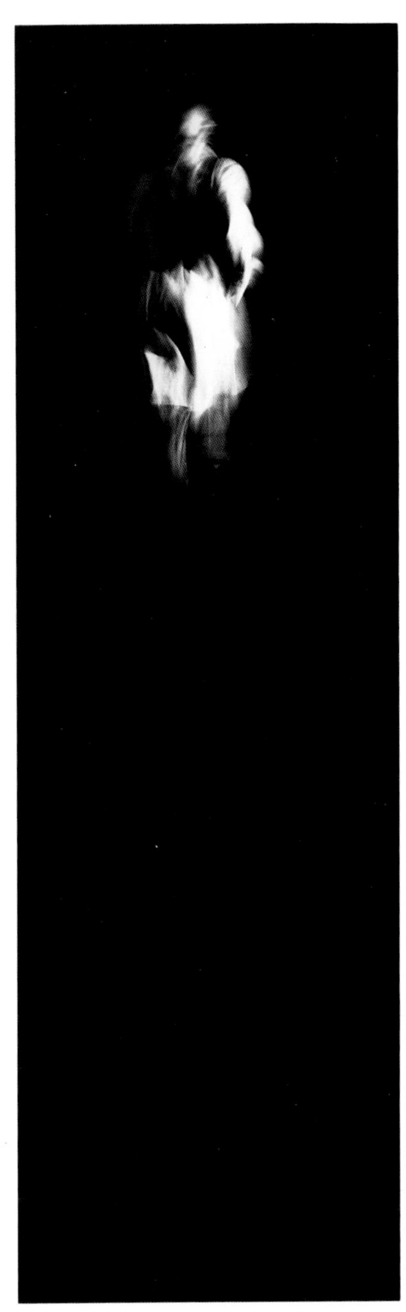

37.

36.
JAY MAISEL

MOSQUE WINDOW, RAYS OF LIGHT

Dye imbibition print (Dye transfer). 1971. Signed and numbered 13/100 in ink on the recto. 8 3/4 x 6 in. Donated by the artist, courtesy Image Bank, New York.

Rays of light suggest spirituality and the sublime in photography. As a representation of what can be seen and felt, but never touched, an image of light can embody our deepest feelings of faith and of hope. Maisel, known for communicating complexity with economy, has contributed a photograph that shows us a passage from darkness into the light.

37.
EILEEN COWIN

RUNNING MAN

Gelatin silver print. 1989. Signed on the verso. 59 1/8 x 18 5/8 in. Donated by the artist, courtesy Jayne Baum Gallery.

There is no foreground and no background, just darkness. A man wearing a glowing coat is in a rush. He could be running from someone. He could be charging toward something. He could be floating upward, from life into death. The only fact Cowin establishes is that this figure has a goal.

38.

38.
HELEN LEVITT

NEW HAMPSHIRE

Gelatin silver print. 1986. Signed, titled, and dated in pencil on the verso. 7 1/4 x 11 3/16 in.
Donated by the artist.

Levitt's photographs have, for decades, communicated to us with a unequivocal candor. Her images of children at play or of people on the street present the simplest activities of everyday life with a fine-tuned awareness of the rich complications of human interaction. This picture speaks quite directly of the universality of nurturing, caring, and support.

39.

39.
ROBERT ADAMS

LONGMONT, COLORADO

Gelatin silver print. 1982. Signed, titled, dated, and numbered 1/30 in pencil with the photographer's copyright stamp on the verso. 18 5/8 x 14 3/4 in.
Donated by the artist, courtesy Fraenkel Gallery.

Colorado's beautiful cottonwood trees have a life span equivalent to that of humans. Although they are brittle, they are also strong and provide nesting habitats for birds. This tree, pictured in the early fall, stood on farmland that, days later, was cleared away for real estate development. Here, as in all of Adams' photographs, the strength of nature is measured against the strength of sheer human will.

40.

40.
JOEL STERNFELD

A MAN WHO JUST COMPLETED
THE LOS ANGELES MARATHON

Chromogenic development print (Ektacolor).
March, 1988. Signed, titled, and dated in ink on the verso.
43 1/2 x 35 in. Donated by the artist,
courtesy Pace/MacGill Gallery.

Sternfeld was photographing in Los Angeles when he came upon an older man who looked remarkably like a figure from a DaVinci anatomical study. Having just successfully completed running a marathon, he obliged Sternfeld and stopped to pose for this portrait. With a medal around his neck and operation scars above each of his knees, his accomplishment is clear. That he stares back at the camera lens so directly strengthens our admiration for his obvious sense of control and will power.

42.

41.

41.
NAN GOLDIN

THE PARENTS ON THE COUCH
AFTER 50 YEARS OF MARRIAGE

Silver dye bleach print (Cibachrome). 1989. Signed, titled, dated, and numbered 2/25 in ink on the verso. 15 1/4 x 23 1/4 in. Donated by the artist, courtesy Pace/MacGill Gallery.

Goldin photographs obsessively, taking pictures of her friends, lovers, and family. Her work is a diary, an emotional document of people who have wandered in and out of her life. Many have since died of AIDS. Here, she pays honor to her parents, who remain a part of her life and act out their love for their daughter.

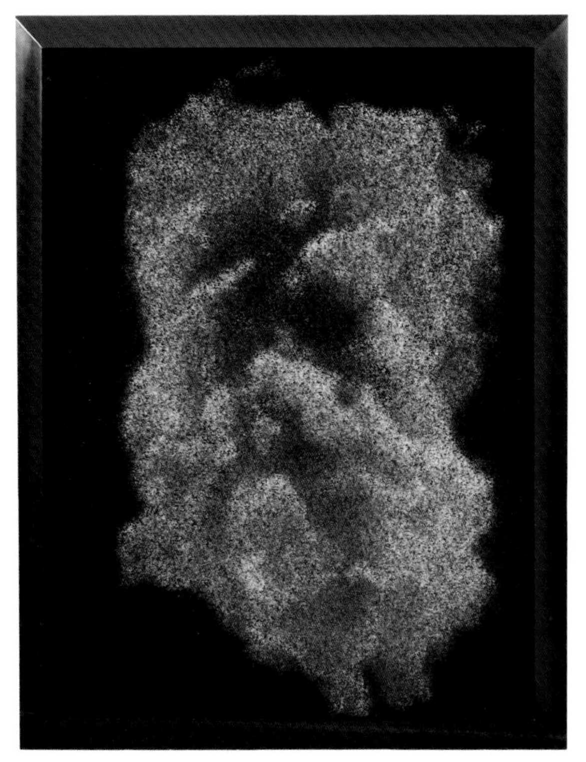

43.

42.
HARRY CALLAHAN

CHICAGO

Gelatin silver print. 1953. Printed later. Signed in pencil in the margin. 7 5/6 x 9 5/8 in. Donated by the artist, courtesy Pace/MacGill Gallery.

This previously unpublished work is from a series of photographs Callahan took of his wife and daughter in the early 1950s. Although it is austere – the empty sky, the harsh sunlight, the blank lawn, two lines of trees – the mood is sweet. With their backs to the sun, the subjects smile for the future, enacting the archetypal snapshot experience that we all have shared and carry within ourselves for the rest of our lives.

43.
ELLEN BROOKS

UNTITLED

Three silver dye bleach prints (Cibachrome). 1986-87. Signed in ink on the verso. 39 3/4 x 29 3/4 in., 24 x 19 3/4 in., and 18 3/4 in. diameter. Donated by the artist.

A bonsai plant. A virus. A fragment of Rock Hudson's face. Three separate photographs combine to suggest how natural beauty becomes unnaturally altered. The miniature tree has been radically, purposefully transfigured. Healthy cells have turned destructive. The loss of a movie star's life to AIDS ends a career but brings the subject of AIDS to a greater public.

44.

44.
JIMMY DE SANA

POWDER #3

Silver dye bleach print (Cibachrome). Signed in pencil on the verso.1986. 11 x 14 in. Donated by the artist, courtesy Pat Hearn Gallery.

De Sana combines three layers of imagery to construct a metaphor. Ocean waves rise and fall until they reach the shore. There, the water sweeps up sand from the beach, only to redeposit it back upon the shore. Against these natural cycles, a diver rises and falls too, his motions implying a third circle. But here, the metaphor ends. The diver's actions appear to be cyclical, like nature's, but they are intentional and proud.

45.

45.

MICHAEL W. DAVIDSON

PHOTOMICROGRAPH OF CRYSTALLINE AZT

Chromogenic development print (Ektacolor). 1989. Signed in ink on the verso. 13 1/2 x 10 in. Donated by the artist, courtesy Department of Chemistry, Institute of Molecular Biophysics, Florida State University.

This seemingly abstract image is about AIDS, but it is not a picture of a person who is ill or a public figure involved in AIDS issues. It's quite different. It is a photomicrograph of AZT, one of the first AIDS medication to prove useful. It is a genuine image of hope.

46.

46.
HIRO

APOLLO-11, 9:32 A.M. 7-16-69,
MAIDEN VOYAGE TO THE MOON

Dye imbibition print (Dye transfer). 1969. Printed in 1984. Signed, stamped, and numbered 4/20 on the verso. 41 x 34 in. Donated by the artist.

A row of spectators watches the launch of Apollo - 11, which four days later was to land on the moon. On July 20, two astronauts walked onto the moon's surface, set up cameras, and were watched by one fifth of the world's population as they planted an American flag and collected moon rock samples. Hiro's image captures the excitement of the lift-off and underscores the bravery and sheer audacity that propel man further into the unknown.

47.

47.
DAVID LEVINTHAL

UNTITLED

Internal dye diffusion transfer print (Polaroid Polacolor ER). 1988. Signed on the verso. 24 x 19 3/4 in. Donated by the artist, courtesy Laurence Miller Gallery.

Our notions of exploration and bravery are based as much upon fantasies as they are upon historical fact. Using children's toys and models from train sets, Levinthal fabricates a scene which, in miniature, encapsulates the tenacity and daring of human achievement. And, if the sources for this image come from Flash Gordon movies as well from NASA, it only adds to our fascination, thrill, and excitement with testing the limits of experience.

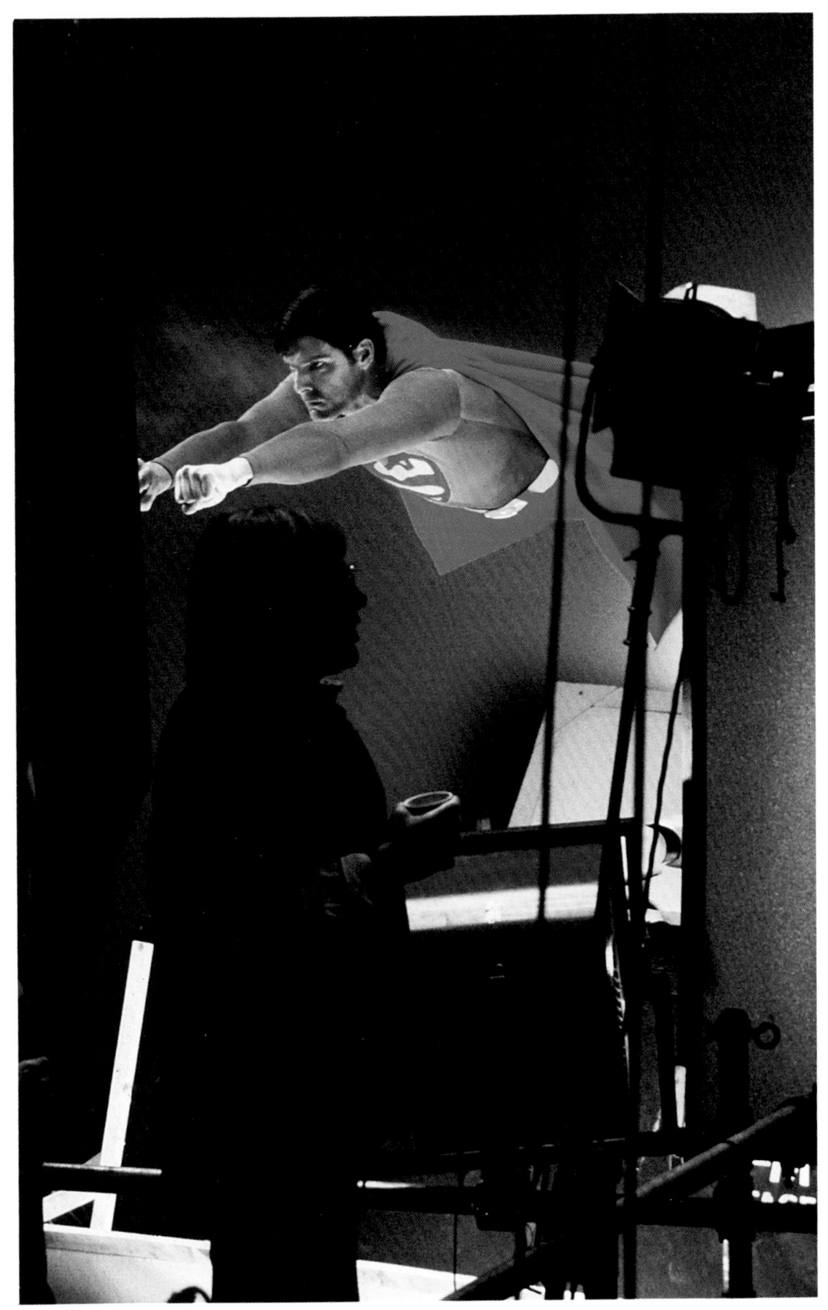

48.

48.
BURT GLINN

SUPERMAN

Chromogenic development print (Ektacolor). 1981. Signed on the verso. 20 x 30 in. Donated by the artist, courtesy Magnum Photos.

Shot on the film set of *Superman*, Glinn's picture makes the tricks necessary to transform a hero into a superhero obvious and amusing. But the photograph is even more interesting once we realize that we long for a miracle to save us from AIDS. Even if we do recognize and understand the fabrication of myths, we still have our reasons to believe in them.

49.

49.
RICHARD PRINCE

UNTITLED (COWBOY)

Chromogenic development print (Ektacolor). 1986. Certificate of authenticity. 27 x 40 in. Donated by the artist, courtesy Barbara Gladstone Gallery.

In the advertising images that fill the media, we are all pictured as indomitable spirits who will, with a bit of help, buy the right products. For the past twelve years, Prince has been re-photographing sections of ads in an effort to understand why their reality is so convincing. This image, extracted from a cigarette ad, makes its subliminal message clear: we are pioneers; we have conquered nature; we are in control. It is no wonder that we pay attention.

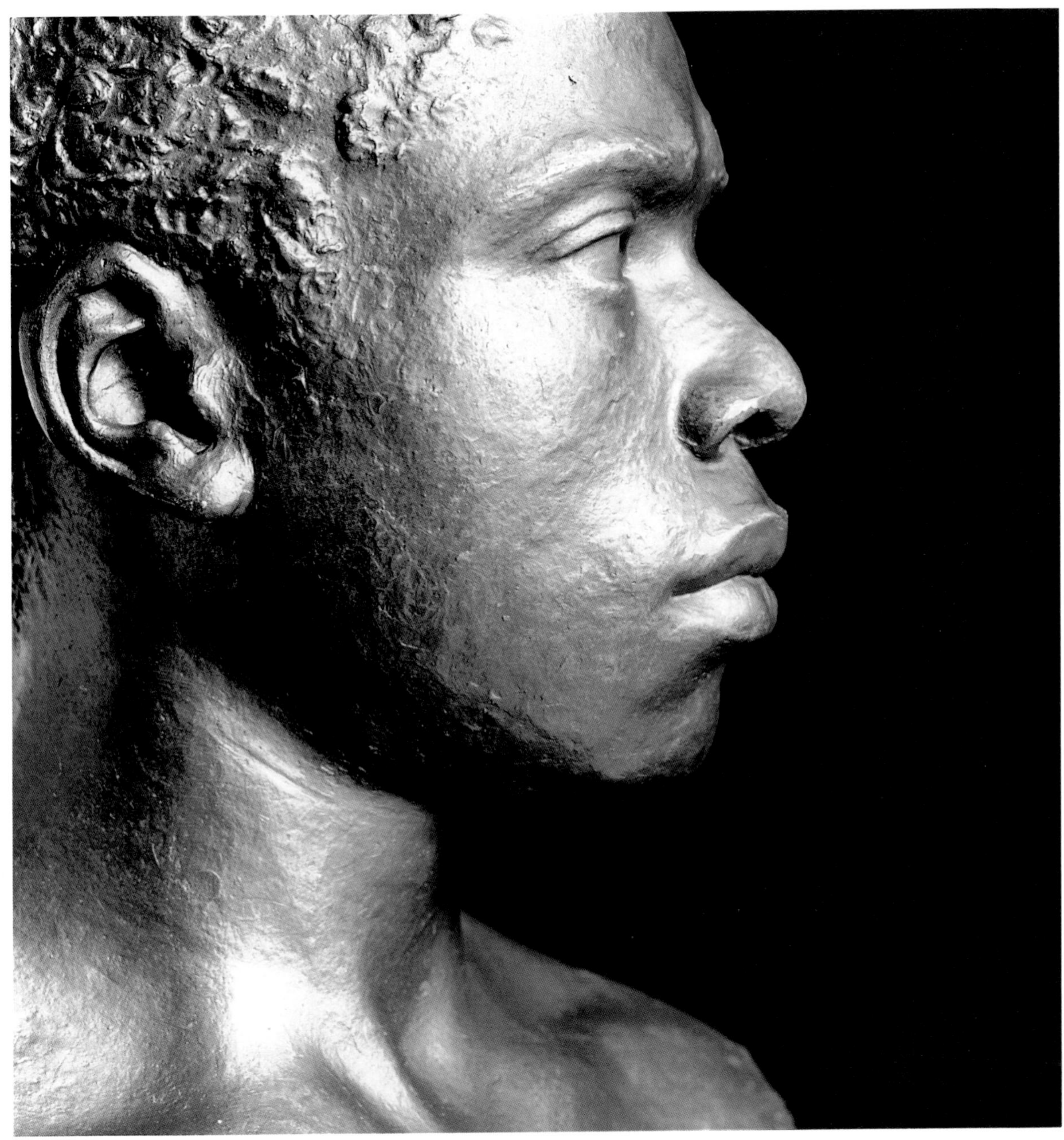

50.

50.
ROBERT MAPPLETHORPE

NEGRO BUST

Gelatin silver print. 1988. Signed, dated, and stamped in ink on the verso. 19 1/4 x 19 1/4 in. Donated by The Robert Mapplethorpe Foundation.

Mapplethorpe, one of the first photographers to support the goals of this project, died of AIDS in 1989. In his still lifes and photographs of flowers, he evolved a signature style that achieved a perfect balance between elegance and meaning. But it was his portraiture – specifically his radically graphic homoerotic images of men – that broke with photographic tradition and represents his important achievement and influence. This image – part still life, part portrait – refers to both aspects of his work, and powerfully addresses the idea of the indomitable spirit.

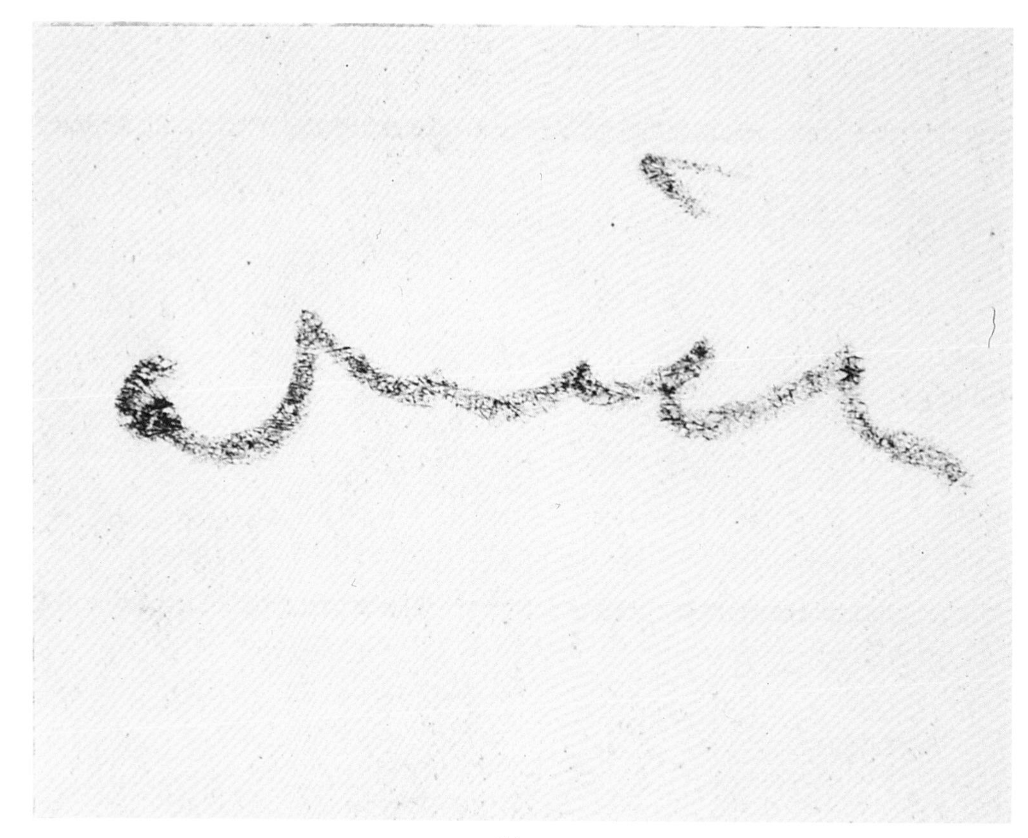

51.

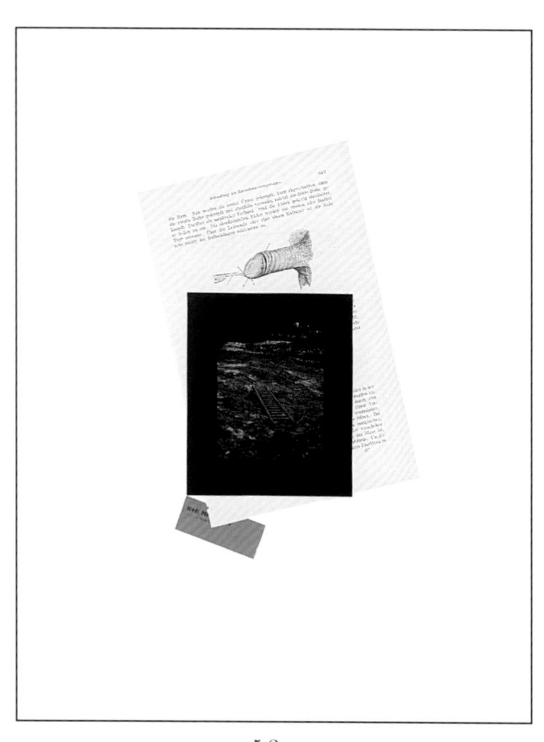

52.

51.
NANCY HELLEBRAND

UNTITLED

Gelatin silver print. 1989. Signed on the verso. 16 x 20 in.
Donated by the artist, courtesy Pace/MacGill Gallery.

In her most recent work, Hellebrand abstracts and photographs fragments of handwriting . The images come from letters she receives, from the notes she writes to herself, and from her children's school papers. The power of communication, so firmly embedded in photography and language, reminds us how we pass along our feelings and reactions from one person to another, from one generation to the next.

52.
JOHN GOSSAGE

FOR BOBBY M.

Collage and gelatin silver print. 1989. Signed, titled, and dated in pencil on the verso. 20 x 16 in.
Donated by the artist, courtesy Castelli Graphics.

This collage is assembled from elements made or collected in Berlin. The illustrated page, from a medical text, refers to the dissemination of scientific knowledge; the photograph of the ladder, to the ingenuity and work needed to reach a goal; the printer's ink sample, to the color of blood. Gossage dedicates this piece to Robert Mapplethorpe.

53.

53.
EVE ARNOLD

ZULU WOMAN WITH CHILD,
SOUTH AFRICA

Gelatin silver print. 1973. Printed later. Signed on the verso. 11 x 16 in. Donated by the of the artist, courtesy Magnum Photos.

Eve Arnold's photograph of three pregnant Zulu women illustrates their determined will to press on with life. "Who could define indomitable spirit more," Arnold asks, "than these three handsome women? To bring black babies into a white South African world is indeed a statement of belief in life and living."

54.

55.

54.
LARRY JOHNSON

CHILE + MEXICO

Two chromogenic development prints (Ektacolor). 1985. Signed in ink on the verso. 20 x 24 in. each. Donated by the artist, courtesy 303 Gallery.

On the surface of the earth, topography separates one region from the next. On maps, the borders that mark off a country from its neighbors are abstractions. The true definition of a nation, as Johnson shows us, is defined by the ideals and struggles of its people.

55.
BILL BURKE

TEMPLE AT TONLE BATI, CAMBODIA

Gelatin silver print. 1988. Signed, titled, and dated in pencil, with copyright stamp on the verso. 16 7/8 x 14 in. Donated by the artist, courtesy Staley Wise Gallery.

The United States bombed Cambodia during the Vietnam War. The Khmer Rouge, under Pol Pot, murdered millions of Cambodians from 1975 until the Vietnamese invasion in 1978. The country has been devastated. The Vietnamese have just withdrawn. There are reports that the Khmer Rouge may return. In Burke's photograph, a Cambodian woman, surrounded by children, prays.

56.

56.
CORNELL CAPA

BORIS PASTERNAK, PEREDELKINO, USSR

Gelatin silver print. 1958. Printed later. Signed, dated, and titled in pencil on the verso. 19 x 14 1/2 in.
Donated by the artist.

Throughout his lifetime, Boris Pasternak – the Russian poet, translator, and novelist – steadfastly disregarded political pressure to write "socially useful" works. In 1958, after the publication of *Doctor Zhivago* in the West, he was awarded the Nobel Prize for Literature. In his homeland, however, his accomplishments and work were denounced. He was forced by Soviet authorities and his peers to reject the prize. Capa's photograph celebrates Pasternak's passion, his spirit, and his willingness to continue to fight for his literary voice.

57.

57.
MARY ELLEN MARK

KENTUCKY

Gelatin silver print. 1988. Signed, titled, and dated in pencil on the verso. 15 $^{1}/_{8}$ x 15 $^{1}/_{8}$ in. Donated by the artist.

Looking like mobilized masks of comedy and tragedy, a pair of twins sit strapped into a stroller. They are infants, reacting to life so instinctively and guilelessly that we respond to their predicament with amusement and with profound respect for their very intense feelings. Mark purposefully reminds us that our reactions to life are intense, and are ours alone, from birth.

58.

58.
MARK COHEN

UNTITLED, SCRANTON, PENNSYLVANIA

Chromogenic development print (Ektacolor). 1987. Signed and titled in ink on the verso. 11 $^{3}/_{4}$ x 17 $^{5}/_{8}$ in. Donated by the artist.

Cohen often photographs as he walks through the streets of Pennsylvania's smaller cities, capturing the gestures of passersby or noticing the incongruous objects that they've left behind. In this sly picture, the discarded packaging reminds us of our ongoing dreams of self-improvement and the poignantly amusing tactics we use to achieve that goal.

59.

59.
WILLIAM WEGMAN

UNTITLED

Internal dye diffusion transfer print (Polaroid Polacolor II). 1988. Signed and dated in ink in the margin. 23 3/4 x 19 3/4 in. Donated by the artist, courtesy Pace/MacGill Gallery.

Wegman's dogs, first the late Weimaraner Man Ray, then Fay Wray, have been elevated to the position of art world celebrities with due cause. In hilarious and often touching series of photographs, they have served as stand-ins for human models and good-naturedly progressed from one absurd pose or predicament to the next. In this photograph, Fay is trapped under a net, her head down in defeat. But we know that by the next picture we see, she will have overcome the obstacle. That fact, in its own funny way, allows us to feel hope for our own predicament.

60.

60.
PETER NAGY

FINDING THE TOMB OF IMHOTEP

Acrylic on canvas. 1989. Signed, titled, and dated in ink on the verso. 48 x 48 in. Donated by the artist, courtesy Jay Gorney Modern Art.

Nagy's painting, which is based upon a Xerox collage, celebrates an indomitable spirit and is accompanied by this statement: Imhotep, the first artist of recorded history, was also an architect, wizard, priest, scribe, and physician ("the father of medicine"). He designed and built the Stepped Pyramid of King Zoser of the Third Dynasty (c. 2750 B.C.) at Saqqara, fifteen miles from modern Cairo. The tomb of Imhotep, believed to be somewhere within the Saqqara complex, has yet to be discovered.

61.

61.
VICTOR SCHRAGER

BLENDER

Chromogenic development print (Ektacolor). 1989.
Signed and numbered 1/5 in pencil on the verso.
59 x 41 in. Donated by the artist.

Throughout the history of civilization, cultures have created objects meant to memorialize birth, the course of life, and human accomplishment. As time passes, the artifacts that survive are assigned specific values; some are treasured as art, others are cherished as memorabilia. In either event, as Schrager shows us, these diverse objects, and the ideas they come to represent, blend together to become part of the tale of culture's survival.

62.

62.
SALLY MANN

UNTITLED

Chromogenic development print (Ektacolor). 1988.
Signed and dated in ink on the verso. 6 x 9 in.
Donated by the artist.

Mann's published images tend to explore the onset of sexuality in adolescents. This picture documents a specific and personal event. Her father, a doctor, was an avid gardner whose thirty acres of flowers, dogwoods, azaleas, and over 300 rhododendrons were justly celebrated. He died on a spring day, just as his cultivated plants began to blossom. This photograph was made after Mann's young daughter wove a bracelet of weeds and wrapped it around her grandfather's wrist, in tribute.

63.

63.
HERB RITTS

SUSPENDED BUBBLE, LOS ANGELES

Gelatin silver print. 1987. Signed, titled, and dated in pencil on the verso. 8 3/16 x 7 7/8 in. Donated by the artist.

The image of the bubble has appeared before in the history of photography in the works of the Photo-Secessionists, who used it as a symbol of mysticism. In our memories of childhood, bubbles mean fun and wonderment. But in this photograph, the bubble takes on a darker, more troubling meaning. Compared with the muscular torso, it is a reminder of the fragility of life.

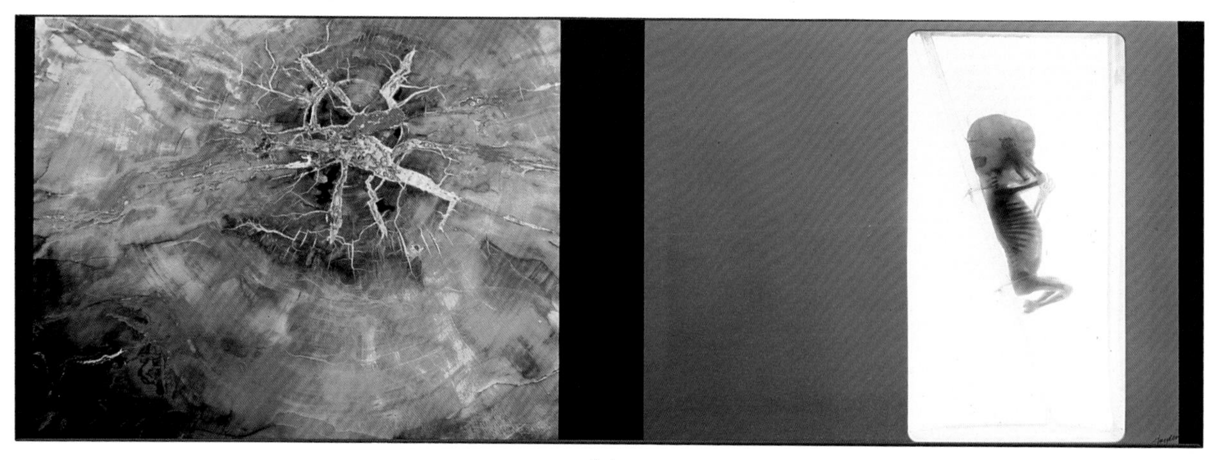

64.

65.

64.
JACQUELINE HAYDEN

A SAINT CRIES

Laminated chromogenic development print (Ektacolor). 1988-89. 16 3/8 x 47 3/8 in. Donated by the artist, courtesy of Brody's Gallery.

The subjects of this dyptich are growth and inquiry. The cross-section of petrified wood, nearly 200 years old, is a record of a life already lived. The X-ray, displaced in a science museum, is a blueprint for a life to come. Hayden reminds us of loss and promise and scientific advancement toward an understanding of life's processes.

65.
TOM BIANCHI

DIVE WITHOUT A SPLASH

Gelatin silver print. 1988. Signed and numbered 1/10 on the recto. 42 x 37 1/2 in. Donated by the artist, courtesy Glenn Dash Gallery.

The diver, balancing control against freedom, is a sheer bundle of energy. He has literally thrown himself into the water, head first, and moves so smoothly that there's barely a ripple. The sensations evoked are shared by us all, personify strength and often go unnoticed in our intense daily lives: the warmth of sunlight, the thrill of risk, the feel of water against skin, the pleasure of play, and a pride of accomplishment.

66.

66.
SARAH CHARLESWORTH

SUBTLE BODY

Laminated silver dye bleach print (Cibachrome). 1989.
Photographer's blind stamp on the recto. 30 x 40 in.
Donated by the artist.

Charlesworth aligns seven photographic images to construct a symbolic spinal column. Each element (snail, lotus, fetus, heart, breast, pitcher, and halo) represents a form of energy. Each is placed to correspond to a specific body part. The work is from a series called "The Academy of Secrets," in which spiritual knowledge is examined, then used to create visual metaphors for the body and the mind.

67.

67.
WALTER IOOSS, JR.

CHRISTIAN

Dye imbibition print (Dye transfer). 1980. Signed in ink on the recto. 19 1/2 x 13 in. Donated by the artist.

For years, Iooss has published in *Sports Illustrated.* It would have seemed appropriate for him to select an image of an athlete hurling himself across a goal line. Instead, he has contributed a personal, touching portrait of his son. That a child's vulnerability and innocence should so clearly echo ours in the face of the AIDS crisis emphasizes how hard we must work to make the future a safe one.

68.

68.
JAMES WELLING

VII, 1987

Internal dye diffusion transfer print (Polaroid Polacolor). 1987. Signed in ink on the verso. 25 5/8 x 19 1/4 in. Donated by the artist, courtesy Jay Gorney Modern Art.

Welling's photograph is beautiful and open-ended. If it seems to address memory or a longing for the past, it is probably because the fabric reminds us of antique display cases, the backgrounds of painters' still lifes, or the draperies upon which sculptors' models posed. If it seems to address the future, perhaps that is because the cloth evokes a landscape in which plants could grow. Above all other possibilities, this photograph speaks as clearly of anticipation as it does of loss.

69.

70.

69.
ALEXANDER LIBERMAN

PICASSO

Gelatin silver print. 1954. Printed later. Photographer's copyright stamp on the verso. 8 5/8 x 13 in. Donated by the artist, courtesy of Andre Emmerich Gallery.

Alexander Liberman is best known as a corporate art director, but he is also a painter, sculptor, and accomplished photographer. It's apt that he should present a portrait of Picasso, who broke and then reinvented the rules of visual art, so that we might better see and understand the intricacy of the world we live in.

71.

70.
HORST P. HORST

CRUCIFIXION, KITZBUEHL (AUSTRIA) CHURCHYARD, WINTER OF 1951

Platinum-palladium print. 1951. Printed later. From the edition of ten with two artists' proofs. Signed on the recto and on the verso. 14 x 11 in. Courtesy of Richard J. Tardiff.

Spiritual journeys often turn into religious pilgrimages, expeditions that are motivated by devotion. These quests are among the most favored subjects in literature, the visual arts, and popular culture. From Chaucer's pilgrims' odyssey, to Horst's trek up to a mountain, to Indiana Jones's perilous itinerary, the goal remains constant: the need to personally encounter the symbols of faith.

71.
ANNIE LEIBOVITZ

MARK MORRIS, NEW YORK CITY

Platinum print. 1989. Signed in pencil on the verso. 17 x 13 3/4 in. Donated by the artist.

Leibovitz's editorial and advertising portraiture is bold, energetic, and revealing. Here, the subject is Mark Morris, who has scandalized and transformed the world of modern dance. In this audacious pose, and in equally bold make-up, Morris's body and gesture manifest fearlessness, daring, and sheer creative nerve.

72.

72.

JOEL-PETER WITKIN

GODS OF EARTH AND HEAVEN

Gelatin silver print. 1988. Signed and dated in pencil on the recto and on the verso. A.P. print outside the edition of 15. 14 3/4 x 14 3/4 in. Donated by the artist, courtesy Pace/MacGill Gallery.

In a tableau that reverberates with Baroque theatricality, Witkin literally constructs a multi-tiered allegory of rebirth. "Five men posed for this image," he says. "When this photograph was taken, the models whose arms circle the man above him suffered from AIDS. Now, a year later, this gentle man is dead. He was my friend, my wife's friend, my son's friend. How fragile, how tender we all are."

73.

74.

73.
ART KANE

UNTITLED

Gelatin silver print. 1985. Signed in ink on the recto.
16 7/8 x 13 7/8 in. Donated by the artist.

Within a single decade, AIDS has radically altered our thoughts and feelings about sexuality. Our growing consciousness of AIDS generates confusion, doubt, fear, and anger. In Kane's photograph, AIDS is the mask that has been forced on us, and our instinctive response is to fight back to save our lives.

74.
JOSEPH STANDART

SYLVAIN LAFORTUNE AND RICK MICHALEK IN CONCERTO SIX TWENTY-TWO

Gelatin silver print. 1989. Signed on the verso.
14 1/2 x 14 1/2 in. Donated by the artist.

Two members of Lar Lubovich's dance company recreate a moment from a work that was choreographed as an homage to people who had died of AIDS. Standart's photograph of the complicated gesture is meant to be suggestive, a reminder of the interlocking nature of all friendships and relationships, and of the continuous cycles of life.

75.

75.
SHEILA METZNER

SPIRIT

Fresson print. 1989. Signed in the margin. 23 x 32 in.
Donated by the artist and Jeffrey Metzner.

Certain moments in life are so perfect, so right, that they seem like a dream. This is how Metzner describes this portrait of her daughter, taken in Santa Fe. The goal was to make an image of energy and spirit: a horse and rider at cliff's edge, bathed in a pink cloud. The odds were stacked against it: an unfamiliar horse, no rider, no reins, no cloud. But, the pink cloud came, the horse and rider took off, and the shutter clicked. The picture remains, a document of what once seemed impossible.

76.

76.
SUSAN MEISELAS

CARNIVAL STRIPPERS

Gelatin silver print. 1973. Printed later. Signed, titled, and dated in pencil on the verso. 15 x 22 1/4 in.
Donated by the artist, courtesy Magnum Photos.

Rather than contribute a photograph of Central America, where Meiselas regularly works, she chose an image of carnival strippers, from one of her earlier published bodies of work. In the context of this project, the picture reads as a parable, underscoring women's equal vulnerability to the AIDS virus and their strength and ability to fight its spread.

77.

77.
LAURIE SIMMONS

ALICE ("YOU CAN LEARN A LOT OF THINGS FROM THE FLOWERS")

Laminated silver dye bleach print (Cibachrome). 1989.
Signed in ink on the verso. 50 x 60 in.
Donated by the artist, courtesy Metro Pictures.

Children's literature is richly populated with characters who are indomitable spirits, heros and heroines who triumph over frightening situations through sheer pluck and perseverance. Simmons, whose works often employ childhood toys as props, reminds us that Alice in Wonderland is, perhaps, the most resourceful and endearing of all these fictional beings. In her trip through the looking glass, Alice triumphs over the cruelties of nature, the irrationality of governments, and the surreal rules that define social interaction, and returns to real life all the better for her very odd experiences.

78.

79.

78.
LOUISE LAWLER

ASSEMBLY

Gelatin silver print. 1984. Signed in pencil with the photographer's copyright stamp on the verso. 28 x 32 in. Donated by the artist, courtesy Metro Pictures.

It was once common to make plaster casts of popular or important sculptures. These copies functioned, in a sense, as photographic reproductions do for us today, by allowing certain experiences to be shared by a wider audience. Lawler's photograph of museum replicas in storage, an assembly of ideals consigned to a warehouse, prompts us to question the symbols and ideals with which we have replaced them.

79.
BARBARA BLOOM

UNTITLED

Silver dye bleach print (Cibachrome). 1986. Signed on the verso. 19 x 10 1/2 and 3 x 4 5/8 in.
Donated by the artist, courtesy Jay Gorney Modern Art.

The works of art that a culture chooses to save and protect form its history. The briefest walk through a museum reminds us of the thoughts and values that have been chosen to represent one century to the next, one people to another. The art that survives is like memory; even in fragmentary form, the feelings, meanings and achievements of the past are carried powerfully into the present.

80.

80.
DOUG AND MIKE STARN

REMBRANDT (HEADS DETAIL)

Toned silver prints, Scotch tape, plexiglass, wood, glue, and metal. 1987-1989. Signed on the verso and on the frame. 60 x 24 in. Donated by the artists, courtesy Stux Gallery.

The subject is Rembrandt, who throughout his career issued multiple versions of his etchings. Perhaps the Starn Twins, who are a multiple themselves, made this portrait to honor Rembrandt's method of working. Perhaps it was made to acknowledge the historical precedent for their own celebrated and repeated use of nearly-identical photographic prints. Or, in the context of this exhibition project, perhaps the work was made to counterpoint the duplication of the AIDS virus with a multiple symbol of art's endurance.

81.

81.
ANNETTE LEMIEUX

MEETING ONE'S MAKER

Gelatin silver print. 1989. Signed in pencil on the verso.
28 x 28 1/4 in. Donated by the artist,
courtesy Josh Baer Gallery.

We make deals with ourselves on a daily basis. Goals are set, motivations are questioned, and accomplishments evaluated in an unvoiced dialogue with our conscience. Lemieux's altered image suggests that if a lifetime's engagement in this process is active and honest, we can ultimately come to terms with life itself, and close the deal with a handshake.

82.
DONALD MOFFETT

I'M NEVER NEVER NEVER LETTING GO

Silver dye bleach transparency with lightbox.
(Cibatransparency). 1989. 25 1/2 x 26 x 4 deep.
Donated by the artist, courtesy Wessel O' Connor, Ltd.

As a member of the activist art collective Gran Fury, Moffett participates in making public art that aims to expose the political attitudes and issues that impede AIDS research and progress. In his own work, the response to AIDS is more personal. The message of this lightbox is not one of defiance, but is an emphatic confirmation of the need for self-reliance and tenacity in this time of AIDS.

82.

83.
HANS NAMUTH

LOS TODOS SANTEROS

Toned gelatin silver print. 1978. Printed later. Signed, titled, dated, and numbered 11/25 in ink on the recto. Titled and dated in pencil on the verso. 13 3/8 x 15 in. Donated by the artist.

Namuth is fascinated by the people of Todos Santos, a small village in the mountains of northwest Guatemala, near the Mexican border. His first visit to Todos Santos was in 1947. Since 1978, he has returned repeatedly, working toward a complete photographic record of the village's inhabitants. Photographing outdoors in a makeshift studio, Namuth assembles a unique document of Mayan village life. In this photograph, two youngsters play for his camera.

83.

84.

84.
SEBASTIAO SALGADO, JR.

ECUADOR

Gelatin silver print. 1978. Signed, dated, and titled on the verso, with the photographer's blind stamp in the margin. 11 7/8 x 17 1/2 in. Donated by the artist, courtesy Ursula Gropper Associates.

Salgado observes the world's social conditions: famine, poverty, and deprivation. Moving through the Third World, he makes impassioned, informative photographs that bring us closer to a reality shared by a majority of the world's population. This image of community caring and support reflects his passion for showing social change as a way to influence each of us.

85.

85.
JOEL MEYEROWITZ

GREENWICH VILLAGE

Gelatin silver print. 1975. Signed, titled, and dated in ink on the verso. 9 x 13 7/16 in. Donated by the artist.

As photographs age, they become evidence of a history. Meyerowitz took this picture fifteen years ago; at the same intersection today, certain things would look the same. People would still caress each other or stand, face upward to the sun. Other things have changed. Buildings have been torn down, some stores have closed. But the biggest change would be unseen. Many of the people who now walk this street do so wondering whether they will live to see it, fifteen years from now.

86.

86.
ALON REININGER

JEFFREY RUBENDALL, AIDS PATIENT, COMING HOME, HOSPICE

Silver dye bleach print (Cibachrome). April 1988.
13 x 20 in. Donated by the artist,
courtesy Contact Press Images.

For eight years, Reininger has dedicatedly photographed all aspects of the AIDS crisis. His images of people living with AIDS, of families coping with the disease, of demonstrations, and of treatment facilities have been published in newspapers and magazines worldwide. Reininger has made an important contribution toward our understanding of the impact that AIDS has on our lives. His photographs are rich in information and make the reality of AIDS less abstract to a public that has not, as yet, been touched by the disease.

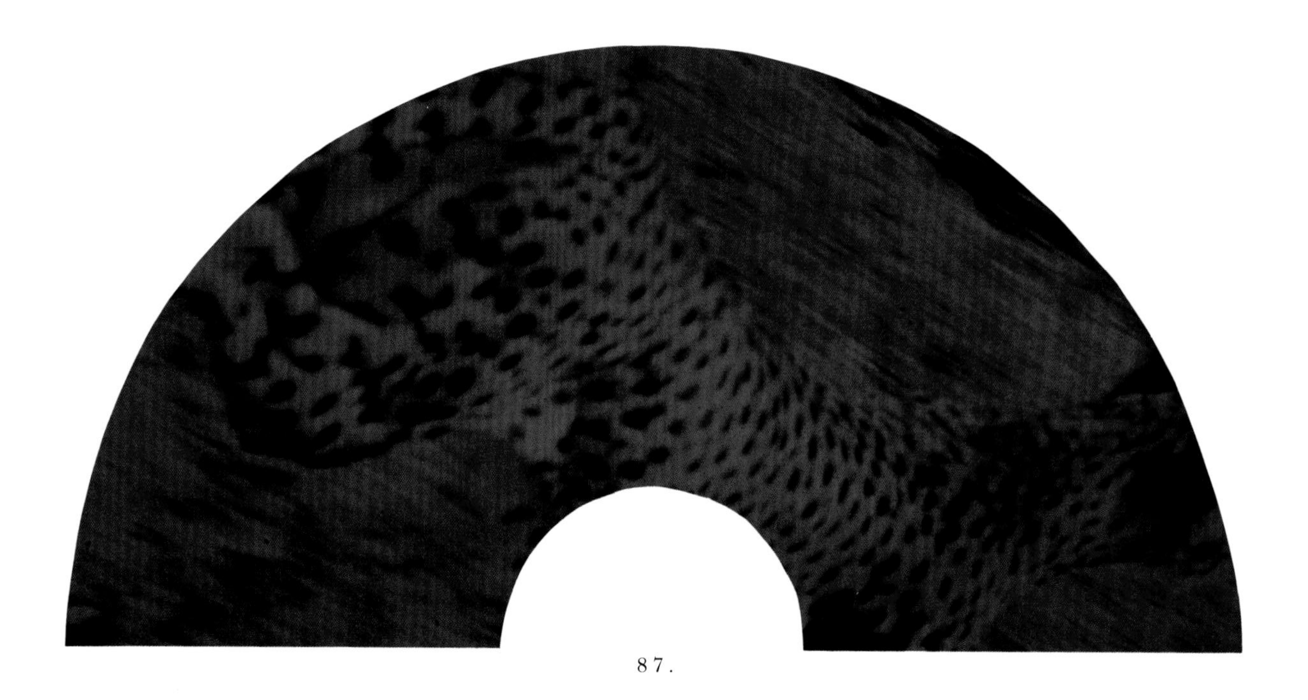

87.

87.
SANDI FELLMAN

PRONATURA #5

Laminated silver dye bleach print (Cibachrome). 1989.
37 x 72 in., arched. Donated by the artist.

In Fellman's work, one of the fastest animals on earth, a cheetah, is seen in motion. Acknowledging that her life and work have been profoundly effected by AIDS, Fellman intentionally chose an animal whose species is endangered as a direct metaphor for human action in the AIDS crisis.

88.

88.
DAVID WOJNAROWICZ

SEX SERIES (TORNADO)

Gelatin silver print. 1989. Signed, titled, dated, and numbered 1/2 on the verso. 18 x 21 1/2.
Donated by the artist, courtesy P.P.O.W Gallery.

Using a combination of text and images, Wojnarowicz directly and symbolically confronts the issues that affect people with AIDS. A text that begins with the description of a safe sex encounter goes on to address political indifference, media inaccuracies, victimization, and sexual repression. The images pit destruction against sensuality, money against scientific investigation, and life against death. Taken together, the pieces merge and give voice to an impassioned affirmation of personal dignity from the frontlines of the battle against AIDS.

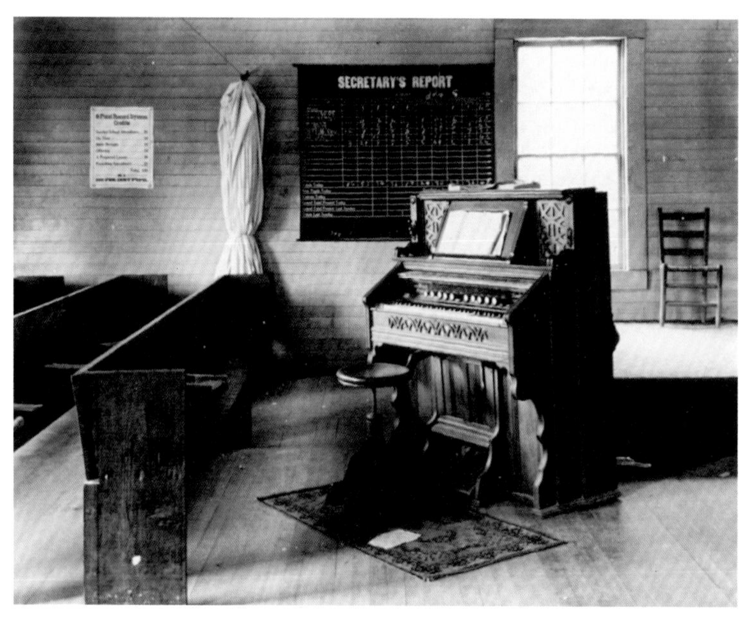

89.

89.
SHERRIE LEVINE

UNTITLED (AFTER WALKER EVANS: 10)

Gelatin silver print. 1981. Signed in pencil on the verso.
7 3/8 x 9 3/8 in. Donated by the artist,
courtesy Mary Boone Gallery.

Through the simple act of appropriating the images of the "masters" of photography, Levine triggers an impassioned debate about the nature of originality. This is a Walker Evans photograph that Levine has copied, then reclaimed the copy as her own. As such, the picture carries two messages. The first speaks of the power of faith, the more obvious subject of the picture. The second message, however, raised by Levine's shrewd tactic, is a confirmation of our experience of the world as our own.

90.

90.
LARRY FINK

UNTITLED

Gelatin silver print. 1987. Signed and dated in pencil with the photographer's copyright stamp on the verso.
14 3/8 x 14 5/8 in. Donated by the artist.

As each of us ages, we begin to revise and reevaluate our responses toward people older than ourselves. Respect for them grows, as we begin to sense the stamina and courage that life has demanded from them and will demand from us when the time comes. Faced with the onset of ailments and the need to maintain dignity in a culture biased toward its youth, the determination to live creatively is both necessary and worthy of attention and praise.

91.

91.
SAL LOPES

AIDS SIGNATURE QUILT

Gelatin silver print. 1988. Signed, titled, and dated in pencil on the verso. 8 5/8 x 13 in. Donated by the artist.

Lopes photographs the section of the AIDS Quilt upon which visitors inscribe their messages to those who have died. The piece of paper reads: *June 8, 1988. Dear Nancy, Here are some wild flowers from our lawn. As you can see, we're behind in the mowing. It was like that in your last visit and you walked around with your trusty camera taking pictures. The rocks are a greeting. It is a Jewish custom. One is from Greece and three are from the driveway! We all go to the white light. You proceed us by a little. Love, Keith.*

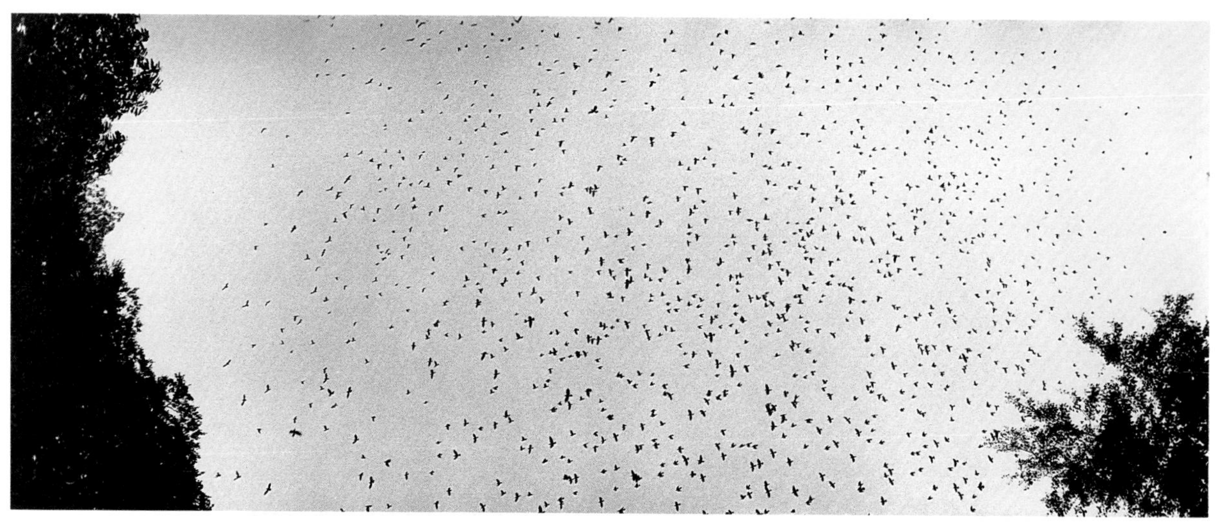

92.

92.
GILLES PERESS

NORTHERN IRELAND

Gelatin silver print. 1989. Signed in pencil on the verso.
15 1/8 x 37 1/2 in. Donated by the artist,
courtesy Magnum Photos.

In our fantasies, photojournalists are romantics who rush from one action spot to the next in search of the perfect, iconic picture. In reality, news photography is now largely left to television crews, and photojournalists are freer to work in depth on stories to which they are personally drawn. Peress has worked in Northern Ireland for twenty years, documenting the country's ongoing religious and political conflicts. This haunting image of birds in flight was taken in County Down.

93.

93.
WILLIAM KLEIN

ACT UP, ATLANTA DEMOCRATIC CONVENTION

Gelatin silver print. 1988. Signed, titled, and dated in pencil on the verso. 12 x 17 7/8 in. Donated by the artist.

ACT UP is a nationwide AIDS activist organization that provokes confrontations to make sure that the issues raised by the AIDS crisis are not silenced or ignored. Klein, known for his graphic and agitated images of city life, captures the full expression of the group's style. Kissing, yelling, laughter, instigation, street theater all are noted in Klein's appreciation of the tactics that need to be employed if the issues affecting AIDS are to remain in the public's eye.

94.

94.
BARBARA KRUGER

UNTITLED

Unique photolithograph. 1989. 50 1/2 x 46 in.
Donated by the artist, courtesy Mary Boone Gallery.

The clock ticks as the fight against AIDS continues. Until a cure is discovered, new cases will be counted, more people will become ill. For the men and women and children who live with AIDS, the will to survive is strong. Their determination to live demands bravery, courage, faith, and an acceptance of the contradictions that life brings.

ALL FILM SEPARATIONS FOR THIS CATALOGUE
WERE PRODUCED ON AGFA MATERIALS,
PROVIDED BY AGFA CORPORATION.

INDEX OF PHOTOGRAPHERS AND ARTISTS IN THE EXHIBITION

NATIONAL BENEFICIARIES

Proceeds from the sale of *The Indomitable Spirit* portfolio, catalogue, poster, and postcards, as well as those from the auction of the works in the exhibition, will be distributed to this following national organizations:

THE NATIONAL COMMUNITY AIDS PARTNERSHIP (NCAP)

The National Community AIDS Partnership (NCAP) is a coalition of national corporations and foundations devoted to funding innovative local community-based AIDS organizations. NCAP was formed in 1988 when ten national corporations and foundations pooled their resources to create a national approach to preventing more people from contracting HIV infection and taking care of those already ill. The NCAP's strategy was to make matching grants to nine communities that promised to raise local matching dollars and to administer the grant award programs to innovative local AIDS groups. One hundred twenty-two community-based AIDS organizations received grants during the first year.

THE AMERICAN FOUNDATION FOR AIDS RESEARCH (AmFAR)

The American Foundation for AIDS Research (AmFAR) is the nation's leading private-sector funding organization dedicated to AIDS research, education, and public-policy projects. AmFAR is dedicated to mobilizing the good will, energy, and generosity of caring Americans to end the AIDS epidemic. Since it started in 1985, AmFAR has awarded $23 million to more than 340 research teams.

PROJECT PERSONNEL
Lisa Cremin, Executive Director
Marvin Heiferman, Exhibition Curator
Ryan Alexander
Jane Axelrod
Eleanor Barefoot
Libby Mc Coy

CONTRIBUTORS

AS OF DECEMBER 15, 1989

CONSERVATORS ($25,000 TO $49,999)

Foundation:
The Charles Engelhard Foundation

SPONSORS ($10,000-$24,999)

Corporate:
Agfa Corporation
Professional Photography Division of Eastman Kodak Company
Fuji Photo Film U.S.A., Inc.
Polaroid Corporation
William Rondina, Inc.
Sotheby's

Private and Foundation:
The Charina Foundation, New York
The Howard Gilman Foundation
The Robert Mapplethorpe Foundation, Inc.
The Robert and Joyce Menschel Foundation

SUPPORTERS ($5,000-$9,999)

Corporate:
Victor Hasselblad Inc.
Polo Ralph Lauren Corporation
Scali, McCabe, Sloves, Inc.

Private and Foundation:
The Joyce Mertz-Gilmore Foundation

CONTRIBUTORS ($2,500-$4,999)

Corporate:
The Image Bank
Leica USA Inc.

Private and Foundation
Mr. and Mrs. Asher B. Edelman

PATRONS ($1,000-$2,499)

Corporate:
Ilford Photo Corporation
Minolta Corporation
Olympus Corporation
Sinar Bron, Inc.

Private and Foundation:
Henrietta Axelrod
Andy Grundberg/Leica Medal of Excellence Award
Joseph Hartney
Jeffrey Johnson
Alan Kornberg
Lynn Lobban
Barry Radick

NATIONAL COLLECTORS COMMITTEE (MINIMUM GIFT OF $1,000)

Gay S. Block
Regina Edelman
John and Lauren Howard
W. M. Hunt
Audrey and Sydney Irmas
Mark and Elizabeth Levine
Ezra Mack
Richard Menschel
Robert and Joyce Menschel
Marjorie and Leonard Vernon
Thomas Walther
Michael and Jane Wilson
Suzanne Winsberg

FRIENDS ($500-$999)

Corporate:
The American Society of Magazine Photographers

Private and Foundation:
James Garcia
Stephen Harty

NATIONAL DEALERS COMMITTEE (MINIMUM GIFT OF $500)

Jeanne Adams, The Ansel Adams Gallery
Castelli Graphics
Keith de Lellis Fine Art
Ronald Feldman Fine Art
The Fraenkel Gallery
Monah Gettner, Hyperion Press
Howard Greenberg, Photofind Gallery
Tom Jacobson
Hans P. Kraus, Jr.
Harry Lunn, Jr., Lunn Ltd.
Curt Marcus Gallery
Robert Mann, fotomann
Lee Marks Fine Art, Inc.
Meyers/Bloom Gallery
Laurence Miller Gallery
Howard Reed, Robert Miller Gallery, Inc.
Douglas Walla, Kent Fine Art
The Witkin Gallery Inc.

DONORS (UNDER $500)

Corporate:
Bonni Benrubi Fine Art Photographs
Janet Borden, Inc.

Private and Foundation:
Phillip Block
Woodrow and Maria Campbell
Jean-Claude Faby
Giovanni F. Foroni Lo Faro
Robert J. Giard, Jr.
John Hoffee
Deborah Irmas
Peter Musto
Jill Rose
Michael Seltzer
Joseph Standart
Louise H. Stephaich
Geoffrey S. Yarema

CONTRIBUTORS OF GOODS AND SERVICES

AS OF DECEMBER 15, 1989

LEGAL COUNSEL

Milbank, Tweed, Hadley & McCloy:
Suzanne A. Feigert, Jennifer Gaghen, John Halvey, Marylynn Marcinek, and Jay Swanson

FUNDS MANAGEMENT

The New York Community Trust:
Joyce Bove, Robert Edgar, and Karen Metcalf

AUCTIONEERS

Sotheby's:
Erin Crowley, Beth Gates-Warren, William Ruprecht, Kae Konen Jonsons, and Robert Woolley

FINE ART STORAGE AND SHIPPING

Crozier Fine Arts:
Robert Crozier, Michael Dames, Eric Hanson, Thad Meyericks, and Joseph Zuttlieg

PHOTOGRAPHIC SERVICES OR SUPPLIES

The Color Center
Duggal Color Projects
Erizan, Inc.
Everett Labs, White Plains, NY
Eastman Kodak Company
Ken Leiberman Labs
Modernage
Museum Services, Minneapolis
Newman Photographic, Bill Newman
Bill Orcutt
Photo Inc., Minneapolis, William Ash
Polaroid Corporation
Mark Salmon
Sotheby's Photographic Studio
The Ultimate Image, Aaron Klein
Zindman/Fremont

DESIGN

Virginia Edwards
Kemper Johnson
Paul Niski

PRODUCTION OF PRINTED MATERIALS

Lee Goodman Design

PAPER

Roosevelt Paper Company

PRINTING

Philip Morris Companies Inc.
Waterstreet Press

EDITORIAL CONSULTANT

Carole Kismaric

POSTCARDS, POSTERS, AND T-SHIRTS

Fotofolio
Martin Bondell and Julie Galant

FRAMES

Bark Frameworks
Creative Wood Design, Ray Vesy
International Center of Photography
Earl Olsen Framers
Minagawa Art Lines

EXHIBITION GRAPHICS

International Center of Photography

REGISTRARIAL CONSULTANT

3E, Jeffrey Pavelka

PUBLIC RELATIONS

Adams & Rinehart:
Judy Brennan, Bruce Dunbar, Trina Hardiman, Stephanie Huff, Liete Kidd, Jeanne Mackey, Ned Scharfenberg, and John Shannon

ADVERTISING

Ogilvy & Mather
Scali, McCabe, Sloves, Inc.

COMPUTER SOFTWARE

The Haven Corporation
Symantec

ACCOUNTANT

Jarvis W. Irving, C.P.A.

BOOKKEEPER

Tom Stevenson

WE THANK THE FOLLOWING FOR THEIR GENEROUS DONATION OF ENERGY, ADVICE AND TIME:

Advertising Photographers of America
Pierre Apraxine
Christine Argyrakis
Susan Arthur
Lisa Austin
Martin Axon
Eric Baker
Adolf Bauer Inc.
Josh Baer Gallery
Gary Beck
BlumHelman Los Angeles
Mary Boone Gallery
Jessica Brackman
Patricia Branstead
Sam Burneson
Cynthia Cannell
Daniel Canogar
Cornell Capa
Marisa Cardinale
Catherine Chermayeff
Skip Cohen
Larry Condon
Kathy Cooper
Patrick DeMarchelier
Amanda DiGianni
Lisa Dirks
Anne Doherty
Regina Edelman
Virginia Edwards
Cheryl Finley
Christopher Ford
Elizabeth Forst
Fraenkel Gallery
Brenda Freiberg
Anne Gabrielle
Barbara Gladstone Gallery
Jay Gorney Modern Art
Susan Hager
Erika Hansen
Willis Hartshorn
Walter Hardgraves
Katy Hazelwood
John Hoffman
Marvin Hoshino
Peter Howe
William Hunt
Sidney Janis Gallery
Earl Johnson
Kemper Johnson
Lori Kaufman
Jeffrey Kay
Diane Keaton
Herbert Keppler
Stewart Ketchum
Dr. Mathilde Krim
Barbara Kruger
Charles Lahti
Ed Leffingwell
Phyllis Levine
Lieberman & Saul Gallery
Lorence Monk Gallery
Simon Lowinsky Gallery
Lee Marks
Michael Mathews
Debra McLeod
Nancy Megan
Charles Melcher
Metro Pictures
Ed Miliano
Bob Miller
Robert Miller Gallery
Bill Mindlin
Anne Minnich
Pace/MacGill Gallery
Art Presson
Joe Rauch
John Reuter
Peggy Ross
William Rondina
David Schonauer
Peter Schub
Jennifer Sharpe
Jacqueline Slater
Marvin Sloves
Temple D. Smith
Harold Snedcof
Carole Southall
Carol Squiers
Jeanne Stallman
Joseph Strear
Dale Stulz
Ed Sturmer
Michael Ward Stout
Tina Summerlin
David Vena
Joel Wachs
Marilyn Wallen
Richard Weisgrau
Michael Whelan
Suzanne Williams
Michael Wilson
David Wirtz
Eelco Wolf
Tom Wyman
Karen Zani
David Zippel

NATIONAL AIDS ORGANIZATIONS

You can contact the following national organizations for general AIDS-related information. They can also provide you with information about local organizations that will welcome your questions, donations, and volunteering of services.

ACT UP (AIDS COALITION TO UNLEASH POWER)
496 A Hudson Street
Suite G4
New York, New York 10014
212/989-1114

Information and direct political action against AIDS

AIDS NATIONAL INTERFAITH NETWORK
475 Riverside Drive
11th Floor
New York, New York 10115
212/239-8700

Counseling services

AMERICAN CIVIL LIBERTIES UNION (ACLU) AIDS PROJECT
132 West 43rd Street
New York, New York 10036
212/944-9800

Legal services

AMERICAN FOUNDATION FOR AIDS RESEARCH (AMFAR)
1515 Broadway
Suite 3601
New York, New York 10036
212/719-0033
800/458-5231 Experimental treatment hotline for people with AIDS (PWA)

Experimental treatment information, medical research and educational information

CENTERS FOR DISEASE CONTROL
AIDS INFORMATION OFFICE
Atlanta, Georgia 30333
800/342-AIDS Hotline information (English)
800/344-7432 Hotline information (Spanish)

CENTER FOR WOMEN POLICY STUDIES
2000 P Street, N.W.
Suite 508
Washington D.C. 20036
202/872-1770

Women in AIDS clearing house and resource center

COALITION OF HISPANIC HEALTH AND HUMAN SERVICES ORGANIZATIONS (COSSMHO)
1030 15th Street, N.W.
Suite 1053
Washington D.C., 20005
202/371-2100

Information, educational programs

THE FUND FOR HUMAN DIGNITY, INC.
666 Broadway
New York, New York 10012
212/529-1600
800/221-7044 National AIDS Hotline and Crisisline

Counseling and educational materials

LAMBDA LEGAL DEFENSE & EDUCATION FUND
666 Broadway
New York, New York 10012
212/995-8585

Legal services and minority outreach programs

NATIONAL AIDS CLEARINGHOUSE
P.O. Box 6003
Rockville, Maryland 20850
800/458-5231
800/342-AIDS

Hotline referral information

NATIONAL AIDS NETWORK (NAN)
2033 M Street, N.W.
Suite 800
Washington D.C. 20036
202/293-2437

National clearing house for local AIDS education and services programs

NATIONAL ASSOCIATION OF PEOPLE WITH AIDS
P.O. Box 18345
Washington D.C. 20036
202/429-2856

Counseling and specific programs for people with AIDS (PWA)

NATIONAL EDUCATIONAL ASSOCIATION
Health Information Network
100 Colony Square, Suite 200
Atlanta, Georgia 30361
404/875-8819

AIDS and HIV information for educators

NATIONAL COALITION OF BLACK LESBIANS AND GAYS
19641 West Seven Mile Road
Detroit, Michigan 48219
313/897-9079

Educational materials and advocacy programs

NATIONAL LEADERSHIP COALITION ON AIDS
1150 17th Street, N.W.
Suite 202
Washington D.C. 20036
202/429-0930

Corporate and business involvement information

NATIONAL MINORITY AIDS COUNCIL
300 Eye Street, N.E.
Washington D.C. 20002
202/544-1076

Clearinghouse information

NATIONAL URBAN LEAGUE, INC.
500 East 62nd Street
New York, New York 10021
212/310-9110

The National AIDS Minority Information and Education Project

AIDS HOTLINES

Alabama
800/445-3741

Arizona
800/334-1540

Arkansas
800/445-7720

California (Northern)
800/367-2437

Connecticut
203/566-1157

Delaware
302/995-8422

District of Columbia
202/332-AIDS

Florida
800/FLA-AIDS

Georgia
800/551-2728

Hawaii
808/922-1313

Illinois
800/243-2438

Iowa
800/532-3301

Kansas
800/232-0040

Kentucky
800/654-AIDS

Louisiana
800/992-4379

Maine
800/851-AIDS

Maryland
800/638-6252

Massachusetts
800/235-2331

Michigan Detroit Area
800/872-AIDS

Minnesota
800/248-AIDS

Mississippi
800/826-2961

Nebraska
800/782-2437

New Jersey
800/624-2377

New York
800/462-1884

North Dakota
800/592-1861

Ohio
800/332-AIDS

Pennsylvania
800/692-7254

Rhode Island
401/277-6502

South Carolina
800/322-AIDS

South Dakota
800/472-2180

Tennessee
800/342-AIDS

Utah
800/843-9388

801/466-9976

Vermont
800/882-AIDS

Virginia
800/533-4148

West Virginia
800/642-8244

Wisconsin
800/334-AIDS

PORTFOLIO

In conjunction with this exhibition, Photographers + Friends United Against AIDS has published a limited edition portfolio including works by John Baldessari, Chuck Close, Jan Groover, Annette Lemieux, Duane Michals, Richard Prince, Robert Rauschenberg, Cindy Sherman, Bruce Weber, and William Wegman.

The Indomitable Spirit portfolio was made possible by a generous grant from the Charles Engelhard Foundation with additional support from Agfa Corporation.

The portfolio was coordinated by Lisa Cremin, Marvin Heiferman, Susan Lorence, Peter MacGill, Bob Monk, Howard Read, and Brent Sikkema and produced through the cooperative efforts of Martin Axon, Igor Bacht, Adolph Bauer, Inc., Brand X Editions - Bob Blanton and Bill Wygonik, Stuart Einhorn, Everett Corporation, Barbara Gladstone Gallery, Jaylen Lithographers - Steven Schreiber, Margo Kingon, the Professional Photography Division of Eastman Kodak Company, Barbara Kruger, Ken Leiberman Labs, Offset Plate Service, Pace/MacGill Gallery, Matrix Graphics, Metro Pictures, Robert Miller Gallery, Polaroid Corporation, Portfoliobox, Inc., John Reuter, Brent Sikkema Fine Arts, Simon Computer Graphics Ltd., David Smoak, and The Ultimate Image.